THE ABC OF
AVALANCHE
SAFETY

Edward R. LaChapelle

THE MOUNTAINEERS • SEATTLE
SECOND EDITION

The Mountaineers: Organized 1906 "...to explore,
study, preserve, and enjoy the natural beauty of the
Northwest."

7 6 5 4 3
7 6 5

Published by The Mountaineers
1011 S.W. Klickitat Way, Suite 107
Seattle, Washington 98134
Published simultaneously in Canada by
Douglas & McIntyre Ltd.
1615 Venables Street, Vancouver, B.C. V5L 2H1
Copyedited by Edna Dam
Cover: Avalanche in the Karakoram Range, Himalaya
(Galen Rowell photo).
Manufactured in the United States of America

First edition 1961
Reissued 1978
Second edition 1985

Library of Congress Cataloging-in-Publication Data

LaChapelle, Edward R.
  The ABC of avalanche safety.

  Bibliography: p.
  Includes index.
  1. Avalanches.   I. Title   II. Title: Avalanche
safety.
QC929.A8L3   1985   363.3′492   85-21393
ISBN 0-89886-103-9

CONTENTS

EXPLANATION OF TERMS

An *avalanche* is a large mass in motion down a mountainside or over a precipice. According to Webster, an avalanche may consist of snow, rock, earth, or mud. In practice, however, the term is reserved in English-speaking countries almost exclusively for the *snow avalanche.* Other types require additional description, such as "avalanche of rock." The more general term commonly used in the United States is *slide,* which may mean any of the substances mentioned above, unless specifically qualified, as in *snowslide.* The term *slide* is taken to mean "snowslide" only when used in a context where the meaning is unequivocal. *Snowslide* and *avalanche* may be used interchangeably to describe the same phenomenon, the difference being only in their respective Anglo-Saxon and French roots. Sometimes, uninformed users of the terms introduce their own distinctions, as in the case of a motorist on a mountain pass who found the highway blocked by an avalanche. When asked why he had ignored broadcast warnings, he replied, "I heard on the radio there was danger of snowslides. If I had known you were going to have avalanches, I wouldn't have come."

An avalanche can fall only where snow has collected on an inclined surface, usually a mountainside. Among avalanche workers this layer of snow is often referred to as the *snow cover,* a direct translation from the German "Schneedecke." German is the language in which much of the widely used avalanche terminology originated, owing to early Swiss leadership in this field. In the United States, hydrologists like to call the same layer of snow the *snowpack.* The two terms are synonymous.

Avalanches normally recur from time to time in the same mountain locality, called the avalanche *path.* The mean length of time between occurrences is the *return interval.* This path consists of three parts. The *release zone* is the area at top of the path where the avalanche starts; it usually involves the breakaway zone for slab avalanches (see below) and is characterized by accelerating motion. The *track* is the middle part of the path, where steady-state velocity usually prevails unless modified by local terrain variations. There is little or no deposition of avalanched snow in the track. Below the track is the *runout zone* (sometimes called the *deposition zone*); usually less steep than the release zone and track, this is the zone in which avalanche motion decelerates and deposition takes place. These distinctions of path parts are of more than academic interest. A prime rule for safe travel in avalanche terrain is STAY OUT OF THE RELEASE ZONES; hence, it pays to make the physical as well as the linguistic distinction.

Avalanches come in all sizes, ranging from very small ones, called *sluffs* (a spelling corruption of "sloughs"), which by definition do not run more than 150 feet, to very large ones involving millions of tons of snow capable of devastating whole mountainsides. In casual usage the latter kind are sometimes called *climax avalanches,* although scientific workers are careful to reserve the term for avalanches of any size that result from a *se-*

quence of meteorological causes rather than from a single snowstorm. (In the latter case, the scientific term is *direct-action avalanches.*) The two usages for "climax" may apply to the same avalanche, but not necessarily. Avalanches in which only the top layers of snow break loose and slide on an underlying snow surface are *surface avalanches.* Those involving the entire snow cover sliding on the ground, are *full-depth avalanches.* Avalanches on open slopes are *unconfined avalanches.* Those whose tracks lie partly or entirely in gullies or ravines are *channeled.*

Two basic types of avalanches are recognized according to conditions prevailing at the point of origin. The *loose snow avalanche* originates at a point and propagates downhill by dislodging successively larger amounts of poorly cohering snow grains, typically gaining in width as it falls. The behavior of avalanching loose snow is analogous to that of dry sand. On the other hand, when cohesion among snow grains increases, large areas of the release zone may break away all at once in the form of a *slab avalanche.* A distinct, cohesive layer of the snow cover then slides on a clearly defined *gliding surface,* often facilitated by the presence of a weak or cohesionless snow layer called the *lubricating layer.* The division between the sliding slab and the stable snow above and to the sides is called the *fracture line.* These terms for slab avalanche features are direct translations from German equivalents.

More recently, a different nomenclature, which follows long-standing usage for analogous features in soil mechanics, has been introduced in the United States. In this usage the gliding surface is called the *bed surface;* the top fracture line, the *crown surface;* and the side fracture lines, the *flank surfaces.* A separate term is not introduced for the lubricating layer. In both terminologies, the surface of compression failure at the downhill edge of the slab forms a shallow berm, the *stauchwall,* a German label which apparently has no equivalent in English-language soil mechanics. The stauchwall marks the upper edge of snows overridden by the falling slab. Slab avalanches are distinguished as *hard* or *soft* according to whether the slab snow has enough cohesion to remain in lumps as it falls or whether it breaks up into a mass of loose snow. While the exact terminology may vary, the physical distinction of different avalanche types is of great practical importance. Most large avalanches and most of those involving accidents (whether large or small) are slab avalanches. The reason a mountain traveler is exhorted to stay out of the release zones is because disturbance of the snow there may provide the *trigger* to initiate fracturing of a slab.

Avalanches are further classified as *wet* or *dry* according to whether or not liquid water is present in the snow at the point of origin. Knowledge on this point may be uncertain. On the other hand, avalanche debris deposited in the runout zone has distinctly different character according to whether or not liquid water is present in the snow—and the difference is easily recognized. When avalanches fall over long paths, they sometimes originate in dry snow but experience sufficient melt in descent that they form deposits as wet snow. Dry snow falling at appreciable velocities conveys some of the snow particles into the air to form a *dust cloud,* an example of *mixed motion.* If the dust cloud predominates, such avalanches are sometimes called *powder snow avalanches,* or simply *powder avalanches.* If a sufficiently dense aerosol is formed by the snow particles entrained in the air, the dust cloud may behave as an atmospheric turbidity current, rushing ahead of the sliding snow at high velocity and occasionally inflicting heavy damage through *wind blast.*

The snow cover on a mountainside is subjected to gravitational forces which cause gradual deformations as well as the sudden fall of avalanches. Compression of the snow perpendicular to the slope under its own weight is called *settlement.* Internal deformation parallel to the slope is *creep,* while displacement of the entire snow cover along the ground surface is *glide.* On an irregular mountainside, or where snow depth varies, or both, these deformations vary in time and space, thereby inducing stresses in the snow cover. Elastically stored strain energy in the snow may be released to propagate fracturing in the form of a slab avalanche fall or, if the snow layers remain in place, in the form of *glide cracks.* Under certain conditions favorable to glide, the snow cover may slowly accelerate, widening the cracks and making an increasingly rapid transition to avalanche velocities. Japanese investigators have termed this phenomenon the *transavalanche,* a contraction of the term "transition avalanche."

PLATES

 STELLAR CRYSTALS

 COLUMNS

 NEEDLES

 SPATIAL DENDRITES
(COMBINATION OF FEATHERY CRYSTALS)

 CAPPED COLUMNS

 IRREGULAR PARTICLES
(COMPOUNDS OF MICROSCOPIC CRYSTALS)

 GRAUPEL (SOFT HAIL)

 SLEET (ICY SHELL, INSIDE WET)

 HAIL (SOLID ICE)

Fig. 1 —Snow crystal forms

CHAPTER ONE

SNOW AND AVALANCHE BASICS

THE SNOW COVER

The reader is urged to give careful attention to the following fundamentals before proceeding to the practical aspects of hazard evaluation. Though a purely empirical knowledge of snow can serve in many instances, a thorough understanding of the basic physical processes involved is essential to interpret observations intelligently.

Snow Crystal Formation

When atmospheric conditions favor condensation of water vapor at temperatures below freezing, various types of snow crystals form (See Figure 1). Density of newly fallen snow often depends on air temperature as well as crystal type. The lightest snow falls under cold, still conditions. The highest densities are associated with graupel and needle crystals falling at temperatures near freezing.

Formation of the Snow Cover

The snow cover accumulates layer by layer with a resulting stratification that displays the history of the weather variations which occurred during its buildup. With the passage of time, structural and crystalline changes within the snow cover (metamorphism) obscure the original stratification and convert the snow into new forms. The layered structure of the snow is a key factor in avalanche formation. The layers have different strengths, and the bond between two adjacent layers can vary widely. When this bond is weak, the layer above it can slide off the one below—the basic criterion for slab avalanches. Metamorphic changes alter layer and bond strengths with time. These changes may either increase or decrease snow stability, depending on prevailing temperature conditions.

Metamorphism within the snow cover is a continuous process which begins when the snow is deposited and continues until it melts. Destructive, or equi-temperature (ET), metamorphism—the normal type—tends to destroy the original forms of deposited snow crystals, which are thereby gradually converted into rounded, isometric grains of ice. The physical process causing these changes is complex, but transfer of water vapor by sublimation from the tips of the crystals to the more central portions appears to play an important role. Strongly influenced by temperature, the process proceeds rapidly near the freezing point. At extremely low temperatures metamorphism is very slow, and it practically stops below $-40°$ F. Since this process takes place with all types of snow crystals, they all tend to approach the uniform condition of rounded grains. The rate of metamorphism is influenced by pressure as well as temperature, with the weight of additional snowfalls accelerating metamorphism of the layer beneath.

Constructive, or temperature-gradient (TG), metamorphism may also take place in the snow cover. This occurs when ice is transferred from one part of the snow cover to another by water vapor diffusion along temperature gradients. The deposition of this vapor around new centers of crystallization forms ice crystals with quite a different character from those of the original snow. These new crystals tend to assume a scroll or cup shape, appear to be layered, and often grow to several millimeters in diameter. The resulting snow—known as depth hoar or, popularly, sugar snow—is very fragile, losing all cohesion upon collapse and becoming very soft when wet. The conditions required for its formation are a rapid change of temperature with depth (steep temperature gradient), which causes diffusion of water vapor within the snow cover, and air permeability sufficiently high to permit diffusion to take place. These conditions are most common in early winter, when the snow cover is shallow and unconsolidated.

Temperature-gradient (TG) snow plays a very important role in avalanche formation. It is responsible for much of the weakness of snow layers and, sometimes, of layer bonds. It is not necessary for complete crystals of depth hoar to form for the snow to become unstable. Even a partial recrystallization may reduce snow strength enough to cause failure under additional load from new snowfalls or wind drift. As TG metamorphism advances, the snow not only loses strength but becomes stiffer (viscosity increases). This is also important for avalanche formation, because stiffer snow is less able to relieve stresses by internal deformation.

Mechanical Properties of the Snow Cover

Snow is a plastic material having both elastic and viscous properties. Because it is viscous, any snow cover situated on a sloping surface tends to deform internally by downhill flow under the influence of gravity. This behavior is known as creep. The snow cover also slides slowly over the surface of the ground, a phenomenon called glide. Both movements are highly dependent on temperature, for snow is least viscous near the freezing point, but becomes increasingly stiff at lower temperatures. This phenomenon is separate from the stiffening effects of recrystallization discussed above under Formation of the Snow Cover.

The tensile and shear stresses produced by uneven creep and glide of the snow cover are an important factor in avalanche formation. Variations in the strength characteristics of snow are among the widest found in nature. The hardness of wind-packed old snow or frozen firn may be as much as 50,000 times that of light, fluffy powder snow. Snow strength continually changes as a result of metamorphism, but also depends on temperature. When snow is disturbed mechanically, then allowed to set, it undergoes a process known as age hardening. This process is more pronounced at lower temperatures. The greatest source of mechanical disturbance in nature is the wind, and an increase in hardness is always associated with wind-drifted snow.

Thermal Properties of the Snow Cover

Because the mechanical properties of snow are so dependent on temperature, the manner in which heat is lost or gained by the snow cover is of primary importance. There are three basic characteristics of snow which strongly influence its thermal properties. First is the high heat of fusion of ice. For each gram of ice existing at the freezing point, approximately 80 calories are required to convert it to liquid water without any change in temperature. The second is the very low heat conductivity of snow, up to 10,000 times less than that of copper. The third is the presence within the snow cover of water in the form of vapor or liquid, as well as ice. Vapor and liquid water play an important part in heat transfer within the snow cover.

The heat supply at the bottom of the snow pack is relatively limited. A certain amount of heat is stored in the surface layers of earth each summer, and this will melt some of the snow during the winter. If cold weather precedes the first snowfall, however, some of this heat is lost. In any case, an appreciable snow cover insulates the ground surface from external heat exchange. The geothermal and stored heat is sufficient to melt small quantities of snow throughout the winter. The occurrence of melting at the snow-earth interface means that the temperature must stay at the melting point. For this reason the bottom of the snow cover is almost always at a temperature of 0° C (32° F) throughout the Temperate Zones.

Heat is both lost and gained in much larger quantities at the snow surface, and the temperature undergoes wide fluctuations below the freezing point. The temperature of the snow surface, which is composed of solid ice, can never be higher than 0° C, because ice melts above this point. The principal media of heat transfer at the snow surface are air turbulence, long- and short-wave radiation, condensation-evaporation-sublimation, rainfall, and internal conduction. The medium with the largest potential is the air. Heat may be conveyed to or removed from the snow surface in large quantities by the process known as eddy conduction, or the turbulent transfer of heat. This process depends on the motion of air over the snow surface and therefore does not occur in completely still air. The amount of snow that can be melted by a strong, warm wind, such as a Chinook, is much greater than can be melted in a given length of time by any other natural source, including the sun.

Large amounts of energy arrive at the earth's surface in the form of shortwave (visible) radiation from the sun, but up to 90 percent of the shortwave radiation arriving at the surface of fresh snow is turned back by reflection. In contrast, snow both absorbs and radiates longwave (infrared) radiation freely. In fact, among all substances in nature, snow most nearly approaches an ideal black body for longwave radiation, efficiently losing as well as gaining heat through this medium. When skies are clear, snow loses heat to space by longwave radiation, the amount depending on the quantity of water vapor and carbon dioxide in the air, as well as the air temperature. Under overcast conditions, snow will lose heat by longwave radiation to clouds if the cloud temperature is lower than that of the snow surface. When clouds are warmer than the snow surface, the process is reversed and the snow gains heat by longwave radiation. This latter condition occurs most often in spring or summer, when the air and clouds are warm and the melting snow surface cannot rise above 0° C.

The effects of long- and shortwave radiation add algebraically to produce the net radiation balance of the snow surface. The net balance in winter is usually positive (snow gains heat) during the day and negative at night. Occasionally under clear skies at high altitudes in winter, when the sun angle is low, the outgoing longwave radiation may exceed the shortwave radiation absorbed by the snow even at midday, and the snow will actually be cooled while the sun is shining. Maximum positive radiation balance is achieved not on clear days, but under conditions of thin fog or low broken clouds in spring and summer, when both long- and shortwave radiation contribute heat strongly to the snow surface.

The exchange of heat in the snow cover by the medium of liquid water or water vapor has its greatest manifestation in the downward percolation of rainwater. This circumvents snow's normally low conductivity and can warm the entire snow cover, from ground to surface, to a uniform 0° C in a matter of hours.

AVALANCHE CHARACTERISTICS

Two principal types of avalanches—loose snow and slab avalanches—are recognized (Figure 2). The classification is always based on snow characteristics at the point of origin, but modification is often necessary for long avalanches that involve more than one type of snow or more than one method of motion. The distinction between the two types is based on the mechanical character of the snow. Loose snow has relatively little internal cohesion and tends to move as a formless mass. Loose snow avalanches start at a point or over a small area and grow in size as they descend. A

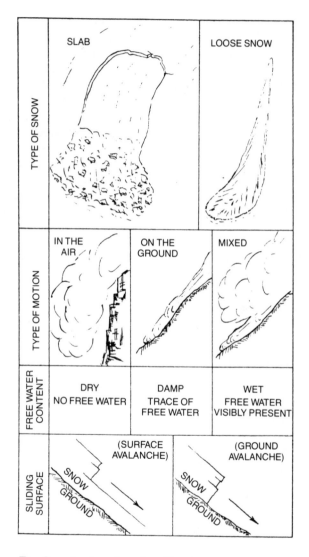

Fig. 2.—Avalanche classification

clearly distinguishable sliding layer is not always present, and the line of demarcation between sliding and stationary snow is often indefinite. Slab avalanches, on the other hand, are made up of snow having a certain degree of cohesiveness, which may vary from only a slight tendency of the crystals to stick together to extremely hard snow which is broken apart only with great difficulty. Regardless of the degree of hardness, the characteristic common to all slab avalanches is that a large area of snow begins to slide at once, instead of starting as a small point as does the loose snow avalanche. A well-defined fracture line where the moving snow blanket breaks away from the stable snow, called the crown, is the positive identifying characteristic. The fracture forms an irregular and often arc-shaped line across the top of the avalanche path, with the face of fracture, called the crown face, perpendicular to the slope. A definite sliding layer, the slab, is usually distinguishable.

Slab avalanches are subdivided into soft and hard slabs. Soft slabs exhibit the typical fracture line but have the general appearance of a loose-snow avalanche once they are in motion. A hard slab contains snow of sufficient cohesion to retain its form in motion. The principal feature identifying the hard slab avalanche is the presence of angular blocks or chunks of snow in the debris, although a hard slab may be completely pulverized if it falls a long distance.

Loose Snow Avalanches

Loose snow avalanches arise when snow accumulates on slopes of steeper angle than its natural angle of repose. The snow on a given slope is made unstable by: (1) deposition of light, fluffy snow under conditions of little wind, (2) reduction of internal cohesion among the snow crystals by metamorphic changes, or (3) lubrication from percolating melt water. Any small disturbance is propagated downward from crystal to crystal, causing the snow to slump downhill towards its natural angle of repose or, if momentum is attained, to slide onto slopes of lesser angle. The disturbance produces a chain reaction as more and more snow is collected in the sliding mass until sufficiently gentle slopes are reached for the moving snow to lose its momentum and come to rest.

The most dangerous loose snow avalanches are those involving wet snow in the spring or summer. Often originating high on the mountains as true loose snow avalanches, these may gather large quantities of snow by the time they reach the valley floor. The weight of wet snow gives them great destructive power even though their velocity may be low.

Slab Avalanches

The slab avalanche is of major concern because it forms the most important source of winter hazard in the mountains. Slab avalanches, in most cases triggered by the victims themselves, are responsible for the great majority of accidents. Slab avalanches are not exclusively associated with any particular type of snow crystal, and especially cannot be correlated with any visible snow characteristic. Wind is an important natural factor in slab formation, as wind-drifted snow commonly develops unstable slabs. But wind alone is not necessary to cause these dangerous slides—

unstable slabs may develop through internal change in the absence of wind.

The tendency of a snow layer to slide depends not only on the character of that layer itself but also on its relation to adjacent layers and on the size and shape of the slope. Assuming that a given snow layer has sufficient internal cohesion to behave as a slab, whether or not it will slide depends on the mechanical character of its attachment to the mountainside. The primary anchorage of a snow layer is to its underlayer, called the bed surface. The strength of the bond depends on the properties of the two layers, the nature of the underlayer surface, the temperature at the interface, and the age of the bond. Gravity tends to pull the snow layer down the mountain. The primary condition of instability is reached when the stress exerted by gravity exceeds the strength of the bed surface anchorage. This may be achieved either by an increase in the stress (increased snow load) or a decrease in the strength of the bond (TG metamorphism, crust disintegration, or meltwater lubrication as examples). However, weakness of the bed surface anchorage is not a sufficient condition for a slide to occur, for a slab is also anchored at the sides, top, and toe. The strength of these anchorages must also be less than the stresses applied to them. The most important peripheral anchor is at the top, where the snow is subjected to tensile (stretching) stress; this is where rupture is most likely to occur following bed surface failure.

If all the forces acting to release a slab exceed the strength of all the anchorages, it will slide. In practice, only certain anchorages may be dangerously stressed, or some or all of them may be stressed close to but not exceeding the breaking point. Any outside trigger which cuts or breaks part of the slab then initiates a sudden redistribution of stresses which may break the anchorages and release an avalanche. The same thing probably happens when a gradual increase in load or decrease in strength causes one of the anchorages to rupture; suddenly increased stresses are thrown onto the other supports and they too break. Failure propagation in the bed surface is thought to be the commonest initiator of slab release. If some of the anchorages are strong enough, they may sustain the slab, as in the common case of a snow slope which cracks but does not slide.

Under the force of gravity, snow on a slope is continually trying to move toward the valley, both by sliding on the ground and by internal deformation (glide and creep). It is the additional combination of stresses created by this glide and creep motion that gives to the slab avalanche its dangerously unpredictable and unstable character. When some triggering agent breaks a slab and relieves creep tension, the reaction of the snow may be very rapid. A whole slope may suddenly shatter into blocks before the slab has a chance to be set in motion. If the snow is very dense and cold, such as in hard slab, the release of tension may be signaled by a sharp cracking sound like a rifle shot. The propagation of a fracture line in snow that is subject to tension from heavy creep is extremely rapid. Such fractures may run faster than the eye can follow for many hundreds of yards across a slope.

If enough time is available, the snow will eventually relieve or redistribute these stresses by internal deformation. The amount of time required depends on the viscosity of the snow. Snow near the freezing point can flow quite readily, and dangerous conditions do not persist for long periods. Thus, danger from warm snowstorms is usually of short duration and the snow quickly stabilizes. As temperature falls, the snow becomes stiffer and creep tension becomes more persistent. As noted above under Formation of the Snow Cover, the progression of TG metamorphism has a similar effect in stiffening the snow. This is the basis for the general rule that the lower the temperature, the longer the avalanche danger may persist.

The formation of unstable slab layers depends on discontinuities in the snow cover. A completely homogeneous snow cover—an even gradation of density, crystal types, and other characteristics from surface to ground—would not likely form a slab avalanche. But each interruption of snowfall causes a change in snow characteristics from one layer to the next. The interface between two layers will usually have less strength than the layers themselves. Therefore a snow cover with sharp discontinuities is a more likely source of slab danger than one that is homogeneous. Hard layers, such as rain crusts, are excellent sliding surfaces and are often the sources of repeated avalanche formation. Moreover, between the bed surface and the slab layer, there often exists a weak layer deposited by light snowfall or surface hoar sublimation. This provides lubrication for the slab through a weak shear bond at the bed surface. As a general rule, snow surfaces exposed to prolonged periods of weathering, no matter what the weather patterns may be, offer a poor bonding surface for a subsequent snowfall and hence often serve as slab avalanche bed surfaces.

Many avalanche slopes reach a state of instability but never fall for lack of a trigger to effect final release. Common natural triggers exterior to the slab or loose snow layer include falling cornices, rolling snowballs, lumps of snow falling from trees, icicles, rockfalls, or small slides. Sluffs that might otherwise be harmless frequently apply enough dynamic stress on the layers over which they run to dislodge larger avalanches. Large avalanches and cornice falls are especially effective triggering agents because they frequently carry enough force to bring down any layers that are not absolutely stable. Explosives are a form of artificial trigger frequently used to effect controlled release of avalanches.

Most avalanche accidents involve the unexpected release of snow slabs triggered by the victims themselves. No doubt many such avalanches never would have fallen had they not been artificially triggered.

Internal triggers involve natural changes in the characteristics of a slab layer. They include temperature changes, overloading by snowfall, and TG metamorphism, any or all of which can alter the stress-strength relationships of a slab beyond its breaking point and so effect release. The operation of these agents is less obvious than the external triggers, but they nevertheless are responsible for the natural release of many slides. The most common internal trigger is fresh snow accumulation, which simultaneously builds a slab and stresses its anchors. In this connection it may be noted that the rate of overloading or deposition of a slab layer also appears to play an important part in avalanche formation.

TERRAIN

Steep gullies and open slopes are natural avalanche paths. Ridges, outcrops, and terraces are natural avalanche barriers. Ridges parallel to the fall line set definite boundaries to an avalanche path, while those running across the fall line halt, slow down, or divert the snow. Ridges also modify the flow of wind so that one side may be stabilized while the other is an accumulation zone for slab. As a practical matter, ridge crests provide the safest routes of travel through avalanche terrain, while rock outcrops may make effective islands of safety.

The most dangerous avalanche path is one with a broad release zone that funnels into a gully. This produces by convergence a deep layer of flowing snow and high velocities. Open slopes produce lower velocities, but large, open slopes permit fractures to run for long distances and very large volumes of snow can be released as falling slabs. The most dangerous avalanche paths in which to be caught are those that run over cliffs or into timber, or that fall into narrow gullies or catchment areas, where burial beneath deep snow accumulations is likely.

Avalanche *accidents* occur on all kinds of terrain. Convex slopes, where creep increases tensile stresses, tend to be active release zones, but many avalanches also release on concave or

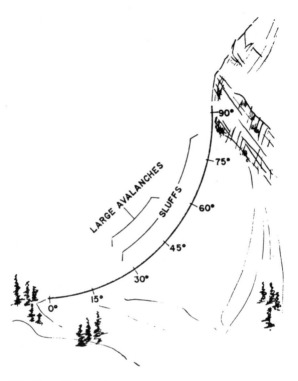

Fig. 3 —Although avalanches may start on slopes ranging from about 20° to 55°, most large avalanches originate in release zones between 30° and 45°. There is a strong concentration of avalanche frequency between 35° and 40°.

plane slopes. The presence in a release zone of a triggering agent (often the victim) is probably a more important factor than slope profile. The slope *angle* at the point of release is also important. Figure 3 summarizes the typical range of angles at which avalanches release. Although avalanches have been observed to start on slopes as shallow as 15°, this is a rare circumstance involving very wet snow. Occasionally, dry snow avalanches will release on slopes between 25° and 30°, but this is not at all common. Most large avalanches start on slopes between 30° and 45°, with a very pronounced occurrence peak between 35° and 40°. People experienced in avalanche control develop a keen sense for slope angle and are able to discriminate high-risk angles from low-risk ones. Less experienced mountain travelers would do well to check slope angles with an inclinometer until they have learned to recognize the most dangerous angles. Skiers often tend to overestimate slope angles by as much as 10° or 15°.

Rough, irregular ground surface tends to retard slides until all the irregularities have been filled in by snowfall or wind drift. Smooth surfaces, such as grass, may permit avalanche formation with only a few inches of snow.

Knowledge of terrain is the key to avalanche safety. Accurate appraisal of snow conditions takes training, experience, and a good source of observational data, but the recognition of avalanche terrain can be easily learned. Safe winter travel in the mountains means, above all, safe route-finding. The avoidance of dangerous slopes, and especially the avalanche release zones, should become a matter of habit for ski tourers and winter mountaineers. The best way to learn safe route-finding is to travel in the company of an experienced avalanche worker. Illustrated slide lectures are also a good introduction. Learning by trial-and-error is the hard, possibly fatal way.

The subtle nuances of terrain recognition can only be learned in the field, but the basic principle is easy to summarize: stay off steep, open slopes. All too often, beginning students of snow and avalanches concentrate their attention on the details of snow metamorphism and internal snow-cover structure, hoping to be able to outguess snow conditions, when the first order of business is to master thoroughly the skills of safe route-finding in avalanche terrain. Again and again, avalanche accident reports are filled with such comments as "The victim took an unsafe line," "The accident party cut right across the release zone," "Mr. X entered the slope at the worst possible point," or, bluntly, "Only an idiot would have chosen such a route." Choose safe routes; it's the best way to stay out of trouble in avalanche terrain.

CHAPTER TWO

PRACTICAL GUIDELINES FOR STABILITY EVALUATION

THE EVIDENCE ABOUT SNOW STABILITY

The winter environment is full of evidence about snow stability, ranging from weather conditions to the actual fall of an avalanche. Not every kind of evidence has equal merit when it comes to judging snow conditions. Some kinds are easy to interpret, others much more difficult. There are three important classes of evidence:

Class I: Direct information about mechanical state of the snow cover. This includes the fall of avalanches through natural or artificial release, propagation of fracturing in snow, snow cover collapse, and failure planes between snow layers initiated by test procedures.

Class II: Indirect information about mechanical state of the snow cover. Most of this evidence is gathered by digging pits in the snow and investigating snow structure. Data include details like layering, slab structure patterns, crystal types, water content, and mechanical strengths.

Class III: Information about meteorological conditions that build the snow cover. These include the commonly observed weather factors like wind, temperature, precipitation, humidity, and

31

cloudiness. Features like new snow density and crystal type, snowfall intensity, and metamorphic changes also fall into this category.

Class I Evidence About Snow Stability

The most reliable evidence about unstable snow is the fall of an avalanche, either witnessed or deduced from observing debris or a fracture line. This may seem obvious, but it needs stating. It is surprising how many beginners are found in an ostrich-like position scrutinizing snow crystals with a hand lens while concrete evidence of snow behavior goes ignored.

An avalanche seen falling says there is danger right *now.* Fresh debris tells of recent instability which may still persist. Older evidence needs more thought. Has the danger period passed, leaving the snow now stable? Or has the older danger been followed by new instability? Crown faces still visible at fracture lines suggest that paths may not yet have been reloaded by new snowfalls. No avalanches at all, especially after a big snowstorm, raises a warning. Has the snow stabilized, or are the avalanche slopes lying in wait for a trigger?

When unstable snow, especially a soft slab, is disturbed, cracks will often propagate for some distance, even on level ground. This is a key indicator of slab avalanche conditions. When such cracks cross the release zone of an avalanche path, a slab may fall. Snow cracks limited to the immediate vicinity of a ski track may not be a sign of danger, but when such cracks shoot out ahead of the skis for 20, 30, or even 50 feet, it's time to stay on safe ground.

The experienced winter traveler constantly

checks for this condition by taking every opportunity to disturb the snow. Kicking a miniature cornice on a gully, the casual flick of a ski pole against a snow cushion, or an extra stamp of the foot on a slope only a few feet long are all ways to see if the snow is under tension and will propagate cracks. Absence of cracking is not a guarantee of no avalanching, but its presence is a serious warning sign.

A weak layer in the snow cover, often depth hoar, can offer poor support to the layers above. When such snow is disturbed, it sometimes collapses with an audible "whumpf." This kind of snow settlement, even on level ground, warns of danger. Similar settling on or in the vicinity of a steep, open slope can easily trigger an avalanche. *Beware of snow that "talks" to you!*

Among the simple mechanical tests used to locate failure planes (shear surfaces) in an unstable slab, the simplest is the "shovel test" (Figure 4). To conduct the test, excavate a pit to the desired test depth, then excavate in the wall of the pit a column of snow on three sides, each about the width of the shovel blade. Working down from the top, insert the shovel at the back of the column and gently pry outward. Watch for the formation of failure planes. In some snow conditions it may help to cut the back of the column first with a snow knife or string. Small shovels are fine, larger ones with a flat blade are better, and a snow knife makes cutting out the snow column faster and easier. An "easy" failure versus a "medium" or "hard" one is a matter of subjective judgment. If the shear plane fails under its own weight without shovel help when the column is exposed, the

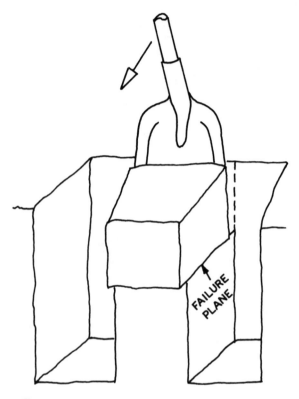

Fig. 4 —The shovel test

snow is definitely unstable. Be careful.

Absence of failure planes does not guarantee no avalanches, nor does their presence assure that an avalanche will fall. But an easily dislodged layer bond in the snow cover is a serious warning sign. Such tests are most effective in the common case of surface instability in relatively new snow.

They are difficult to execute and much less reliable for deep failure planes under a hard slab.

Caution! Although the shovel test is most informative when done in locations near actual release zones, do not conduct it in dangerous terrain; work on a safe slope. The test examines snow structure by creating a miniature slab failure; take care not to create a full-scale specimen.

Class II Evidence About Snow Stability

Indirect evidence about the mechanical state of the snow cover includes the following:

1. Thickness of snow cover. Thickness, the simplest characteristic of the snow cover, tells a lot about stability. A shallow snow cover, usually less than 3 feet, can experience strong TG metamorphism and set the stage for later avalanching by losing mechanical strength. Deep snow, on the other hand, favors ET metamorphism and increasing stability with time, but it fills or covers terrain irregularities, which inhibit avalanche formation, and hence favors surface slab formation.

2. Slab configuration. The slab structure is a combination of layering which puts at least moderately cohesive snow on top of a favorable sliding surface, a weak layer, or a combination of both. The slab layer can range from soft, new snow to old, settled wind slab with the consistency of concrete. The avalanche-forming slab configuration does not depend on any specific *kind* of snow in the slab layer. It depends on the proper *combination* of slab, weak layer (failure plane), and sliding surface. A snow pit's key function for checking stability is to locate slab structure patterns.

The weak layer may be low-density new snow,

surface hoar (very common), some graupel to serve as ball bearings, or a water-saturated layer in wet snow. Sometimes no distinct weak layer can be seen in the pit wall, but a poor bond between one snow layer and another may still exist. The shovel test (Figure 4) can help locate weak layers and bonds.

The sliding surface is often a buried crust or ice layer. It may be an old, smooth, windblown surface or simply a snow layer with a higher density and strength than the slab above. The sliding surface of a previous avalanche is also a good candidate. Sometimes, especially with wet-snow avalanches, the sliding surface is the ground and the slab is the whole snow cover. Many cold-snow avalanches *start* by sliding *on* weak depth hoar but end up sliding on the ground, when their motion causes the depth hoar to collapse.

3. Snow crystal types. The different types of snow crystals are also useful indicators of snow stability. Fine-grained, settled old snow (ET metamorphism) tends to be stable if it extends throughout the snow cover, though it can still build slabs if a sufficiently weak layer lies underneath. *TG snow in any state of development is a universal warning sign.* Such snow means loss of strength and gain in viscosity (stiffness), both of which contribute strongly to slab avalanche formation. Depth hoar, the end-product of metamorphism, is always a danger sign, and at the very least it makes snow behavior difficult to predict. Fresh loading on depth hoar by snowfall or wind drifting generates dangerous instability whose exact character is very difficult to evaluate. When depth hoar is around, be careful!

4. Mechanical strength. The mechanical strength of snow, such as ram resistance, gives useful information about snow cover behavior. Instruments for making such observations are not readily available to the casual investigator with one exception—the snow shovel. A surprising amount of information can be obtained just by digging a snow pit. One's kinesthetic sense, or "feel," of how snow reacts to a shovel is a rich source of knowledge about snow strength and texture. In many cases, all the rest of the observation routine to log layer characteristics may just be window dressing; the key information may be obtained by the time the digging is finished.

Snow produced by ET metamorphism has a solid, cohesive feel. TG snow, on the other hand, has a more friable texture that disintegrates more easily and tends to be brittle even when soft. Poorly consolidated, often unstable snow shovels easily and can be scooped up or broken with little effort. Snow settled enough to gain strength and stability is harder work to shovel. Each shovelful has to be spaded or pried loose.

The fine points of the kinesthetic sense are hard to convey in print, but experience quickly makes the differences clear. The habit of digging frequent, shallow, quick snow pits to check surface conditions, coupled with close observation of stability (Class I data), is one of the best ways to gain a confident understanding of avalanche formation.

5. Temperature. Temperature affects snow behavior in many ways. Some are subtle, requiring careful measurement and interpretation. Others are obvious and provide much of the important temperature information about stability.

The biggest temperature distinction is whether the snow is cold (sub-freezing) or at the melting point with some liquid water present. Cold snow does not change very fast; at low temperatures avalanche danger may persist for a long time. Close to the melting point, but still sub-freezing, the snow changes rapidly, and high avalanche danger does not last long. With meltwater or rain present, many snow characteristics change so quickly that metamorphic processes are short-circuited. In wet snow extreme avalanche danger may develop quickly but usually does not last more than a few hours.

Strong temperature gradients within the snow cover warn of declining snow strength. Their effects may not become evident immediately, but they show a *trend* toward instability. The effects of temperature gradients are most pronounced in early winter; they diminish toward spring, as the snow cover warms.

Class III Evidence About Snow Stability

Snowfalls are the key meteorological evidence for avalanche formation. The bigger the snow-storm, the bigger and more likely the avalanches. A foot or more of new snow is always a warning sign. Three feet in a single storm is getting down to serious avalanche business, and really big blizzards that dump 6 feet or more in a very few days can generate large avalanches everywhere. Even more important than the quantity is the rate of fall, or snowfall intensity (S.I.). When slopes are loaded quickly, whether by precipitation or wind drifting, the snow cover cannot adjust fast enough to the new burden. As a result, instability rapidly increases. Even a substantial amount of snow, up to several feet, may not cause much danger if it falls over a long time. The critical loading rate for the common soft slab formation seems to be around 1 inch of snow per hour.

An even better measure of loading is precipitation intensity (P.I.), the rate of snow accumulation measured in its water equivalent (the amount of water that would result from melting the snow). The critical P.I. is about 0.1 inch of water equivalent per hour. Any sustained snowfall above this rate accompanied by high winds practically guarantees some sort of avalanching.

The kind of crystals that make up a snowfall also can affect avalanche formation (Figure 1). Ordinary stellar or dendritic crystals do not particularly favor large avalanches unless they are broken and packed by the wind. When coated with rime, they are much more likely to build soft slabs; fully developed graupel (pellet snow) can build dangerous slabs in thick layers or lubricating layers in thin ones. Crystal types like needles or plates, which pack to higher densities, favor slab formation. In fact, any kind of snow crystals that create atypical new snow densities can favor avalanching. Typical densities run around 10% water equivalent. Below about 5%, the very light snow tends to slide off as loose sluffs, whereas densities above 12% to 15% contribute strongly to building dangerous slabs.

Wind controls the distribution of snow on the mountainside. Wind loading on lee slopes is a prime cause of high snowfall intensity and snow depths, hence of avalanche formation. The critical velocity for dangerous wind transport is around 12 to 15 mph, varying a bit with snow type. Winds of

15 to 40 mph are avalanche builders. Above 55 to 60 mph in colder climates avalanches are much less likely to form; most slopes become either scoured or heavily wind-packed. In coastal areas with warmer climates and wet, heavy snow, major storms with hurricane-force winds can lead to serious avalanching. Wind direction is very important because it determines *which* slopes will be loaded and where cornices will form.

Air temperature and humidity affect the kind of snow crystals formed during storms. Air temperature and radiation conditions (see Thermal Properties of the Snow Cover in Chapter One) also control the heat balance of the snow surface. Many temperature effects on snow are complex and difficult to interpret. A few, however, are simple. A rapid *change* in air temperature, either up or down, affects stability. A sudden, sharp cooling can put thermal stresses on hard slabs. Such a temperature drop from above to below freezing can trigger wet snow releases as it first occurs, followed by stability as the snow freezes solid. A sudden rise from sub-freezing to melting frequently provokes avalanches if the initially cold snow was weak and unstable to begin with. The temperature *trend* during a snowstorm is important. A falling temperature brings with it decreasing new snow density and a more stable snow deposit. A rising temperature, on the other hand (the so-called "inverted storm"), brings initial low snow densities to form a good failure surface for the subsequent higher density accumulation, the ideal soft slab configuration. The air temperature at or just before the onset of snowfall is also important. New snow bonds poorly to a previously cold surface, but sticks much better to relatively warm though still sub-freezing snow.

An important general weather factor in avalanche formation is *rapid change* of any kind. A sudden onset of a snowstorm, changes in temperature as noted above, a shift from snowfall to rain, or high winds springing up to cause rapid loading of lee slopes are all warnings of avalanche development. A quick change in wind direction or velocity during a storm, an abrupt change in snow crystal types, a shift in radiation conditions as clouds move in or out, all can cause or set the stage for avalanches. Always be alert to sudden weather changes in the winter, consider what the effects will be on the snow cover, and proceed with extra caution when a stable weather period of any sort comes to an end. Pay especial attention to the onset of rain or rapid thaw conditions, for these produce the most profound changes in previously cold snow. Rain in midwinter can change safe slopes to deadly ones in a matter of minutes.

The Chain of Cause-and-Effect in Avalanche Formation

In any given area the terrain is fixed and determines *where* avalanches can fall. *Whether* and *when* they will fall is determined by a chain of cause-and-effect that runs from the weather systems that generate snowfalls through the complex evolution of snow cover structure to the final mechanical state of loads and weakness, stresses and strains, that determine the degree of instability at a given time and place. The observer follows this chain by observing nature from Class III through Class II to Class I evidence about snow stability. The farther one gets down this chain, the more direct and unambiguous is the evidence: Class I data come closest to answering the question "will it avalanche" with a simple YES or NO. The warning signs are clear and easy to interpret. Moving back up the chain to Class II data, the answer is more often a "maybe," and the questions begin to multiply. A wider range of factors, such as slab structure, failure planes, and relative layer strengths have to be weighed against one another. Backing up even farther, to Class III data, the many nuances of wind, snowfall, temperature, crystal types, radiation effects, and their interactions together form a complex network of cause and effect. The same question has to be answered, "well, perhaps if...," or "not unless X is followed by Y," or "probably, if A, B, and C occur, but not D."

The lesson is clear. The hard decisions about snow stability are best made when based on Class I data. (This is why ski patrols in developed ski areas spend so much time using bombs and artillery; the answers thereby obtained about snow stability are 98% unambiguous.) Increase the data uncertainty (Class II, or even more so, Class III) and the answers start getting fuzzy. Evaluations become more general and less specific: "A rising hazard may occur in the Southern Rockies by tomorrow night." The fuzzier the answers, the wider the safety margin that must be allowed in practical decisions.

Ideally, stability evaluation should focus on the least uncertain class of evidence. In the real world, some data from all classes are usually considered, with the balance of emphasis shifting according to locale, season, and snow patterns. Sometimes the evidence from one class is overwhelming. Three feet of new snow overnight, no matter what else happens, practically screams, "avalanche." Depth hoar so fragile it flows out of a pit wall like dry sand tells of a snow cover on the point of collapse. The really big hazard situations are often obvious. It is the condition of marginal stability that so often traps the unwary skier and that requires careful analysis. Recognizing avalanche danger is always a synthesis of many kinds of evidence, some of it not always consciously perceived. The principles of this synthesis, along with some practical rules, are outlined in the next section of this chapter.

ANALYZING THE EVIDENCE

The Nature of Avalanche Forecasting

A stability evaluation deals with the *current* state of the snow cover but coupled with weather forecasts, it attempts to foresee *future* avalanche conditions. In either case, the act of evaluating, or forecasting, snow stability should be *an ongoing process,* not a last-minute or one-time event. The skier who is about to cross an avalanche path and suddenly decides to investigate snow conditions with a pit, think about weather effects, or scan the horizon for recent avalanches has started the process too late…much too late. At the very minimum, conditions should have been considered before the tour started that morning. Better would have been two or three days, or even a week, of paying attention to weather developments.

Accurate knowledge about snow conditions is built up bit by bit, adding a little meteorology here, some snow stratigraphy there, salting the mixture with a few shovel tests, and stirring it to form tentative conclusions that can be checked against actual avalanche occurrence. The experienced forecaster is always thinking about snow conditions and considering how today's weather may change them tomorrow. The experienced forecaster *always has an opinion about snow stability,* no matter how uncertain or tenuous, which can be checked against actual snow behavior and modified by further observations. As emphasized earlier, this modification proceeds most accurately when based on Class I evidence, but where this is not available, Class II or Class III evidence is sought. The farther back up the chain of cause-and-effect one must go, the more diverse and numerous must be the data to improve the stability opinion. The evaluator is always looking for extra information, one more bit of evidence to reinforce or disprove the snow stability estimate. In Chapter Four, examples of actual stability analyses by experienced hands make this process clear.

The Two Problems in Avalanche Forecasting

There is a useful distinction between *absolute* and *conditional* instability of the snow cover. Absolute instability means the snow has reached a point where widespread natural avalanche releases *will* occur. The conditions producing this state are usually obvious, such as a big storm with a lot of new snow, a sudden onset of rain in midwinter, or a severe episode of depth hoar formation followed by strong wind drifting. Even beginners have little trouble predicting what is going to happen in such circumstances. Much more difficult to deal with is conditional instability. This means that a slab avalanche structure has formed in the snow cover but will actually generate avalanches *only when an adequate triggering force is supplied.* Evaluating stability then becomes much tougher, for the key question then becomes: "How big a triggering force is needed?" If only an earthquake or large explosion will dislodge the snow, it is stable for practical purposes. But if the weight of a skier can start a slab moving, the danger is obviously high. Yet the external appearance of the snow cover may be the same for both cases. This is the heart of the matter: *A really reliable decision about the actual danger during conditional instability can only be made on the basis of Class I information.* Anything else is a probability estimate, guesswork of varying reliability. For absolute instability, Class II and Class III data will do the job because the probabilities are overwhelming. But if the situation is conditional and you don't know the trigger size required, allow a wide safety margin and get more information from observed avalanche falls, test skiing, or evidence of fracture propagation. In the case of key decisions (e.g., to cross an avalanche slope or not), even the shovel test begins to assume Class II uncertainty.

When approaching the challenge of a stability evaluation, the first question to ask is which of the two problems are you facing: absolute or conditional instability?

Some Basic Rules About Evaluating Stability

1. Avalanche forecasting is an evolutionary process. Each forecast, each stability evaluation, ideally begins with the first snowfall of winter.

2. It is not difficult to recognize a general pattern of unstable snow in a given mountain area. Doing so rapidly becomes more difficult, however, as the area of concern narrows down to a specific avalanche path at a specific time.

3. Class I data are the easiest to interpret. Class II data are more complicated. Class III data are often open to many alternative interpretations. The best way to beat confusing data is by building redundancy, i.e., by gathering more than one line of evidence about snow stability.

4. There is a fundamental asymmetry to understanding avalanches. It is much easier to recognize conditions leading to 100% certainty of avalanches than it is to recognize that the snow is 100% stable.

Some Basic Rules About Snow

1. Any snow or weather condition that departs from normal may decrease snow stability. An important corollary is that any departure from the normal course of ET metamorphism in the snow cover can set the stage for slab avalanches.

2. Absolute instability occurs only a very small percentage of the time, typically for a total of a few hours each winter. Conditional instability can persist much longer, as long as several weeks in cold climates when depth hoar is in the snow cover.

3. The exposed snow surface breeds instabil-

ity. Weathering of the snow surface adversely affects the bonding of the next snowfall. The longer the period of weathering, the worse the bond.

4. Formation of wet-snow avalanches in the spring usually is governed by the *net* heat balance at the snow surface. This balance is determined by several factors, not just by sunlight (see Chapter 1).

5. *Most avalanches are caused by a rapid change in the thermal or mechanical energy state of the snow cover.*

SPECIFIC GUIDELINES FOR SPECIFIC SITUATIONS

Soft Slab Avalanches

Soft slabs involve low-density, and hence mostly new, snow. They form as a direct result of snowfalls and can quickly reach dangerous instability which, however, normally does not last long. Soft slab avalanches usually involve surface layers of new snow and are directly associated with fresh snowfalls. They are probably the commonest source of danger in the mountains. *Beware of soft slab avalanche danger during and after big winter storms.* If temperatures remain only a few degrees below freezing, the snow stabilizes rapidly, often accompanied by visible signs of settling. At lower temperatures the danger can persist longer, even for days.

Many snowstorms do not produce soft slab danger in the absence of certain other key weather factors. The most important of these is high precipitation intensity. An inch or more of water equivalent (around 10 inches of snow) falling at rates of 0.1 inch per hour or more, accompanied by strong winds, reliably produces avalanche danger. Heavy (high-density) new snow is especially avalanche prone. If the storm deposit falls on a deep snow cover with a smooth surface, soft slab formation can be widespread, sometimes with little regard to wind direction below timberline. Heavily rimed snow crystals strongly favor dangerous soft slabs, while unrimed crystals tend to build very shallow and hence less dangerous slab avalanches.

Extensive sluffing during a storm stabilizes avalanche slopes and inhibits slab formation. Midstorm sluffing may not always be visible because it is obscured by later snowfall. Soft slabs are especially amenable to ski testing because the ski tracks penetrate the slab layer and disrupt it. From this standpoint, soft slabs can be recognized from Class I evidence without much difficulty. Experienced observers can often recognize soft slab snow conditions just on the basis of the "feel" while skiing, even without actual fracturing or avalanche release on test slopes. The Class III evidence, such as the precipitation and snow type effects outlined above, also are reasonably easy to interpret. It is the Class II evidence which gives little help in recognizing soft slab conditions. The slab structure patterns in new snow can be so subtle that they go unrecognized in a pit wall or lie outside the measuring range of typical test instruments like the ram penetrometer.

Hard Slab Avalanches

Of all avalanche types, hard slabs are the most dangerous and unpredictable in behavior. Such snow is strong enough to support appreciable load or withstand weak triggering forces without release. Dislodgement may occur unexpectedly on slopes on which previous skiing or other disturbance has failed to have any effect. This contrasts with the more "touchy" behavior of soft slabs, which usually are stabilized or released by skiing. Hard slabs are particularly sensitive to temperature changes, and a sudden fall in temperature may greatly increase their instability.

The primary agent in developing hard slabs is snow transport by high winds. Average wind velocities of 25 to 50 mph are commonly associated with this form of hazard. Strong wind transport can create very heavy lee deposition zones during light snowfalls, or even during fair weather. It is not uncommon to find slabs 6 feet thick forming in a few hours. This same heavy wind transport of snow tends to localize the hard slab danger on favorable lee slopes, in contrast with the more ubiquitous soft slab danger.

The weak layers underneath hard slabs that form the failure planes frequently consist of depth hoar or old, buried surface hoar. These make hard slab conditions especially difficult to analyze, for failure can occur unpredictably. The high mechanical strength of thick, dense snow layers that make up a hard slab favors strong anchorage to the terrain. Even with a very weak layer underneath, such snow may support a heavy accumulation built up over an extended time before failure actually occurs and an avalanche falls. This is a very difficult situation to recognize, because no class of evidence about snow stability tells very much. Class III data may be stretched out over time and therefore difficult to interpret unless an overwhelming event like major wind drifting occurs. Class II data may give useful information such as an obvious depth hoar layer, but deep, hard snow offers practical obstacles to an easy pit excavation, and when a pit is dug, the failure plane can be overlooked if it is thin and indistinct. Even Class I data is not of much help in evaluating hard slab danger. Actual hard slab releases tend to be erratic indicators; ski testing is ineffective; slab cracking is hard to initiate; and shovel tests are impractical. *Do not expect ordinary ski testing routines to reveal hard slab danger.* Some serious avalanche accidents have happened through misunderstanding this principle. The most reliable way to check hard slab danger is to blast the slope in question with a heavy charge of explosives, though even this is not 100% certain.

A hard slab with an unstable failure plane located deep within the snow cover is the most difficult avalanche situation to deal with. Careful attention to all the evidence can point to instability, but reliable conclusions are hard to reach. When a hard slab is suspected, the best policy is to play safe and practice conservative routefinding to stay away from release zones.

Wet Snow Avalanches

Wet snow avalanches fall when free water lubricates or weakens snow layers with some latent instability. They do not occur in snow at temperatures below the freezing point. As long as subfreezing temperatures exist, percolating water is refrozen. Melt water or rain is a very efficient transporter of heat through the snow, however, and deep snow layers may be quickly warmed up when sufficient water is available.

Wet snow avalanches may fall either as slabs or as loose snow, depending on snow conditions, but the primary cause is the sudden intrusion of a large amount of water in the snow. Winter rainstorms are one source of wet avalanche danger, and are common in the maritime climate of the Pacific Coast ranges. Melting by solar radiation, warm winds, or both, is another cause. Melting due to radiation depends on the net radiation balance. During clear, dry weather, longwave radiation cooling of the snow surface tends to counteract the heat from the sun, and late winter or spring snow may remain stable during clear days, only to develop a wet avalanche cycle on a warm, hazy or cloudy day, when the actual radiation heating of the snow is higher and may persist all night as well as during daylight hours.

Wet snow avalanche danger is most acute when heavy melting or rain introduces free water into a cold, dry, and poorly consolidated snow layer. Hence late-season snowstorms are apt to be followed by a wet slide cycle, especially on south-facing slopes, if the next day is sunny. Deep falls of new snow in midwinter that turn to rain at the end of the storm are a similar source of danger.

A layer of depth hoar at the bottom of a snow cover may precipitate large wet ground avalanches in the spring, when percolating meltwater reaches this unstable layer and further weakens it, while at the same time reducing the strength properties of the overlying layers.

Sunballs rolling down a slope are indicators of rapid changes taking place in the snow. They may be forerunners of wet slide activity, though not always. The danger usually is not high if the sun-balls are small and penetrate only a few inches into the surface layer. But if these balls grow in size during the day and eventually achieve the form of large snow "wheels" that penetrate deeply into the snow, then wet snow avalanching may be imminent.

Impervious layers in the snow cover, such as an old rain crust, favor wet slab formation by trapping meltwater where it can provide extra lubrication.

Old, settled snow, or summer firn snow, is much less likely to cause wet slides. Snow which has been warmed up to the freezing point for some time is usually well-stabilized and able to resist the effect of percolating water.

Avalanche Dangers in Summer Mountaineering

At high altitudes, winter avalanche conditions persist into summer. In addition, summer mountaineering presents its own hazards.

1. Old summer snow, or firn, normally is highly stable. Snow avalanche danger (as contrasted with that from ice avalanches) usually result from summer snowstorms. Warmer air and intense solar radiation can cause much more rapid changes following a storm than occur in winter. Damp or wet snow avalanches—both loose snow and slab—may follow a fresh snowfall. The danger from damp or wet slabs may in some circumstances persist for several days, even in warm weather.

2. Wet snow avalanche activity will cease when the snow freezes on a clear night (even with air

temperature above freezing). These avalanches may fall at any time on overcast nights, or in wet, rainy weather, for the snow then does not freeze.

3. The bergschrund at the head of a glacier sometimes serves to create a slab avalanche fracture line, presumably due to the additional stresses introduced by glacier motion.

4. Snow avalanches on a glacier offer a peculiar source of hazard, for even a small and otherwise harmless slide can carry a climber into a crevasse and bury him very deeply. Consider carefully the possible consequences before risking a crossing of an avalanche slope with crevasses below.

5. When climbing cliffs or steep gullies, beware of hidden snow fields above which may discharge unexpected slides, especially on a sunny afternoon.

6. At higher elevations, prolonged snowstorms may create winter snow conditions and typical winter avalanching in midsummer. In such situations the previous general outline of winter avalanche formation applies. The principal modifying factor is the much greater heat available in summer from solar radiation.

7. In the high mountain ranges of Alaska or the Himalayas, winter is truly present the year around, and snow avalanches must be expected at any season. A peculiar hazard arises from the great size of the avalanches that may fall from these huge peaks. Such avalanches may fall many thousands of feet from entire mountain faces and run for miles across glaciers or valleys below. Such slides have been observed to ascend the opposite mountain walls for thousands of feet.

Selecting campsites safe from such avalanches is sometimes difficult.

8. Ice avalanches belong to a separate category. They occur on the steep ice cascades of glaciers or under hanging glaciers and ice cliffs. The location is usually restricted and usually obvious, except in poor visibility. Their fall, on the other hand, is often impossible to predict, for collapse of a tottering serac or the fracturing of an ice cliff depends as much on glacier motion as it does on such processes as internal melting. Zones of frequent avalanche activity are usually apparent from broken ice debris of previous falls. Unlike snow avalanche accidents, in which the slides are usually started by the victims, ice avalanche accidents generally result from a natural fall. The basic safety precaution, therefore, is to minimize exposure to the hazard. Climbing parties should traverse passages beneath ice avalanche zones as quickly as possible. Avoid bivouacs or rest stops in such exposed zones. There is sometimes a reduction of ice avalanche activity at night, when the ice freezes up, but this is often not the case when glacier motion is vigorous.

CHAPTER THREE

SAFETY RULES AND RESCUE

MINIMIZING AVALANCHE RISKS

When traveling in avalanche terrain:

1. *Never travel alone.*

2. Always conduct the march in such a fashion that only *one person at a time* is exposed to avalanche danger. This is the *first cardinal rule* for ski touring, and one too often neglected. If one person is buried by an avalanche, his chances of rescue may be good if his companions are free to search for him or go for help. If an entire party is trapped by an avalanche, its chance of survival is greatly reduced.

3. Stay off avalanche paths and, especially, out of release zones. This is the *second cardinal rule* for ski touring. Accident records show that *most avalanche victims start the avalanches themselves.* Cases where unsuspecting victims have been overwhelmed by a slide falling naturally from above are very much in the minority. *The safest route* around an avalanche path is over the top, along ridges. The next safest route is along the valley floor, at the foot of the avalanche path. The *most dangerous route* is on the avalanche path, where the passage of a skier may trigger the release of an avalanche that otherwise would not have occurred.

4. Do not camp, bivouac, or make rest stops at the foot of an avalanche path. The probability of getting caught by a natural fall rises rapidly when exposure is prolonged. The chances of getting caught while you are moving are very much smaller.

5. On winter tours in the backcountry, carry electronic rescue transceivers and some emergency rescue equipment. (See below.)

6. The greatest danger exists during or immediately after a heavy snowfall or prolonged periods of high wind. Stay out of hazardous areas at these times. (Danger may persist for many days if temperatures are low.)

7. Do not assume a slope is safe just because it did not slide when the first person crossed it. Especially in the case of hard slabs and low temperatures, avalanche release may be triggered unexpectedly at some later time, even after considerable traffic on the slope. There is one case on record where an avalanche trapped the thirty-third man of a military patrol crossing a dangerous slope. In another case, a fatality occurred when the late afternoon release of a hard slab trapped a victim on a slope which several skiers had used as a ski run all day.

8. Beware of lee areas, the slopes beneath cornices, and deep drifts, especially those with a convex profile. These are all prime locations for avalanche fracture zones.

9. Do not assume that avalanches are confined to open slopes. Dense timber is usually good protection, but open or scattered timber stands may not necessarily hold the snow. This is particularly true in the Rocky Mountain region, where depth

hoar formation is common in early winter. Several avalanche fatalities in Colorado have resulted from release of slab avalanches on timbered slopes.

10. Most dangerous avalanches originate on slopes between 30° and 45°. Be careful on slopes within this range.

11. When you set forth on a tour, take advantage of local knowledge of snow and avalanche indications. Professional ski patrol members or U.S. Forest Service snow rangers often can give you the latest information based on the most complete snow and weather records available.

12. Test skiing is an attempt to artificially release avalanches on selected small slopes by skiing. It serves as a field test of snow stability to check the conclusions of hazard forecasting. The reaction of snow under skis constantly provide information on the physical processes taking place in the snow cover. Test skiing can detect snow which is tending to form slabs and create an impending hazard, particularly during storms. A key to successful test skiing is the selection of test slopes which accurately represent the snow conditions found on the larger and more dangerous avalanche paths. Cracks which form in the snow with the passage of skis are the best indicators of developing slab avalanche danger. Breaks in the snow immediately adjacent to the skis are not necessarily a danger sign; the weight of the skier may simply be cracking the snow locally. Breaks or cracks which run ahead of the skis are more clearly a warning of slab avalanche formation. *Warning!* Test skiing is one of the most useful tools for detecting avalanche danger, but it can be

hazardous if done carelessly. The following precautions are mandatory:

- Work only on small, short slopes with a safe outrun.
- *Never* test ski alone.
- Only *one* person on the test slope at a time.
- *Always* cut slopes at the *top*.
- Do not attempt test skiing unless you are a competent skier.
- Adopt the safety precautions outlined on the following pages.
- Remember that test skiing is most effective in soft, surface slabs — it may not work in hard slabs. Deep, unstable layers in the snow, like depth hoar at the bottom of a hard slab, may remain undisturbed by passage of a skier on the surface, but still cause a major slab release later on.

13. Crossing an avalanche slope in the back-country involves a certain calculated risk. You may be unable even to guess whether or not the slope will slide, but you usually can estimate *what will happen to you if it does slide* while you are on it. Taking a calculated risk may be justified if the slope is short and not likely to bury you deeply at the bottom. But if the slope is long, funnels into a gully instead of fanning out, falls over cliffs, or would carry you into rocks or trees at the bottom, the risk may be more foolhardy than calculated. Ask not only "will it slide?" but also "what will happen if it does slide?"

14. Any travel in avalanche terrain involves *some* risk. Keep this risk to a minimum and always play the odds in your favor. If there is a choice of two different routes, take the least dangerous one,

even if both seem to offer low hazard. A lot of seemingly small risks, if repeated, can add up in the avalanche's favor. One chance in a hundred of getting caught may seem a small risk. But if you repeat this one hundred times, the odds become something like 6 to 4 in favor of the avalanche; repeat a risk of two chances in one hundred a hundred times and the odds in favor of the avalanche increase to about 7 to 1. Old hands at snow safety work learn this principle so well that they take the safest line in avalanche terrain even when they know the snow is stable. This is a good rule for all winter travelers in the mountains.

If you must cross an avalanche slope:

1. Remove the wrist loops of your ski poles.

2. Unhitch the safety straps from your skis so they won't be tied to you if you are carried down in a slide. If your bindings are of the non-release type, loosen them so you can get out of your skis easily. In a recent major accident in Canada, ten skiers were caught in a huge slab avalanche. All were carried down and buried. Two were able to dig themselves out and free a third skier buried close to the surface. The other seven were deeply buried and perished; all of those seven were attached to their skis by safety straps; the survivors were not. The lesson is obvious.

3. Close up your clothing, don hat and mittens, and raise your parka hood. If buried in the snow, your chances of survival will be much better if snow doesn't get inside your clothes to cause chill.

4. Loosen rucksack straps so it can be dumped quickly if necessary.

5. Wear an avalanche cord if one is available.

Tie one end to your belt and let it trail out behind you. If you bring down a slide the cord has a good, though not guaranteed, chance of floating on the surface even though you are buried. If your party is using electronic rescue transceivers, make sure by audible check that they are all working in the transmit mode. Also make sure that they are securely attached inside your clothing, where forces generated by the avalanche will not tear them away.

6. Gain some measure of security by climbing or descending the fall line on foot instead of traversing the questionable slope on skis. A fall line track is less likely to cut a slab anchor than is a diagonal or horizontal ski track. In highly unstable situations, there may be little to gain by going on foot, and the mobility offered by skis in deep snow may recommend them in spite of the risk of cutting the slope. Wallowing through chest-deep snow in the middle of an avalanche path is not an experience to be relished.

7. Take advantage of natural protection offered by the terrain. Rock outcrops, clumps of trees, or ridges may offer islands of safety in the avalanche path. Lay your route between these and, if on skis, try to make rapid downhill traverses which will carry you to the next safe spot even if the snow does start to slide.

8. Cross a suspected slope so that *only one party member at a time* is exposed to avalanche danger. The other members should watch the person crossing so they can plot his probable course in case a slide is started and he is swept down and buried.

If you are caught in an avalanche:

1. Call out so other members of your party can observe your course in case you are buried.

2. Discard poles, skis, and rucksack.

3. Try to swim in the snow in order to stay on the surface. Try also to work your way to one side of the moving snow. In a large or fast-moving avalanche such efforts will probably be of little avail, but they may save your life in a smaller one.

4. If you find these efforts are not helping, cover your face with your hands. This will help keep snow out of your nose and mouth, and allow you to clear a breathing space if you are buried. As the avalanche slows down, try to maintain some space around your chest to allow respiration. Avalanche snow often becomes very hard as soon as it stops moving. Your chest may be constricted and your arms pinned wherever you find them when the snow comes to rest.

5. If you are buried, try to avoid panic. Frantic and fruitless efforts to free yourself will only consume valuable oxygen. Stern self-control is essential to survival.

6. In soft snow you may be able to dig yourself out, or at least make room to breathe. If you try to dig out, make sure you dig up toward the surface. Persons buried in an avalanche have actually lost their sense of direction and tried to dig down. Also be aware that while you may hear sounds from the surface very clearly, rescuers can seldom hear you. Snow is an effective sound insulator. Although this insulating quality works in both directions, into and out of the snow, the *perception* of sounds by buried persons and by those on the

surface is entirely different owing to the large difference in background noise.

7. Many avalanche survivors are rescued immediately by their companions because they have a hand, foot, or piece of equipment protruding from the avalanche debris. If you think you are coming to rest near the surface, try to reach out a hand or thrust up a foot or ski (but keep one hand free to clear space around your nose and mouth).

RESCUE BY SURVIVORS

Memorize these ten steps. If you are a surviving member of a party caught in an avalanche, the lives of your buried comrades may depend on what you do in the next few minutes.

1. *Don't panic. Check for further slide danger* —pick a safe escape route in case of a repeat.

2. *Mark last-seen point.* Mark the point on the avalanche path where the victim was last seen as he was carried down by the snow. This will narrow the area of your search and that of the rescue party. Use a firmly planted ski, pole, or large branch which will not be lost under a subsequent snowfall.

3. *Quick search.* If there are only two or three survivors, they must make a quick but careful search of the avalanche before going for help. If at all possible, one person should be left at the accident site to continue the search and guide the rescue party.

4. *Search surface below last-seen point.* Search the surface of the avalanche for evidence of the victim or clues to his location. Mark the location of any pieces of his equipment you may

find—these may provide additional indicators of the path taken by the flowing snow. Search carefully and kick up the snow to uncover anything which may lie just beneath the surface. If the party is using electronic rescue transceivers, switch the survivors' units to "receive" and commence searching.

5. *Sole survivor.* If you are the sole survivor, you must still make a thorough search of the avalanche before going for help. This may seem obvious, but it is a rule all too often neglected. Even the simplest search may enable you to find the victim and free him alive.

6. *Thorough search.* If a rescue party can be summoned only after several hours or longer, the survivors must concentrate on making as thorough a search as possible with their own resources. The chances of a buried victim being recovered alive diminish rapidly after the first half hour.

7. *Probing.* If the initial search fails, begin probing with the heel of your ski, inverted ski pole, or collapsible probe below the last-seen point. Trees, ledges, benches, or other terrain features which have caught the snow are most likely places to search. If there are several survivors, probing of likely spots can continue until a rescue party arrives. If you are alone, you will have to decide when to break off the search and seek help, depending on how far away it is.

8. *Send for help.* If there are several survivors, send only two. The remaining survivors must search for the victim in the meantime. If it will take a half hour or more for help to reach the site, and the avalanche is not too large, the victim may have a

better chance if everyone remains to search. This is a difficult decision which depends on individual circumstances.

9. *Going for help.* When going for help, travel carefully, avoiding avalanche dangers and injuries from trying to ski too fast. The victim's chance of survival may depend on your getting through. Mark your route, especially if fresh snow is falling, so you can find your way back. Try to avoid complete exhaustion. The rescue party normally will *expect you to guide them back to the accident site* unless its location is absolutely clear.

10. *Care of the victim.* When the victim is found, immediately give first aid for suffocation and hypothermia. Free the nose and mouth of snow, clear the chest, and administer mouth-to-mouth resuscitation unless the victim is able to breathe freely without assistance. Cardiopulmonary resuscitation should be applied in the absence of breathing and pulse, only by those trained in its use. It should not be interrupted once begun. Clean out snow from inside the clothing and place the victim in a sleeping bag with external sources of heat. Persons buried for any length of time in snow are apt to suffer severely from hypothermia and will need effective rewarming. Other injuries should be treated according to standard first aid practices.

ORGANIZED RESCUE ACTIONS

In his book *The Avalanche Enigma,* Colin Fraser remarks that "to be in an avalanche is to have at least one foot in the grave, and more usually both." Statistics fully bear him out. Records kept in Switzerland over a 37-year period ending in 1977 show that an average of 25 persons per year died in avalanches. Less complete records suggest a figure of about 100 per year for the entire European Alps. In Japan, for the 56-year period ending in 1974, the average was 28 persons per year. In the United States, fortunately, there are considerably fewer fatalities, averaging 6 per year for the 25 years ending in 1975. The trend, though, is rising: for the decade ending in 1984, U.S. fatalities averaged 15 per year.

Even more instructive are the survival statistics. In Switzerland, where the records are most complete, 1,347 people survived partial or complete avalanche burial over a recent 30-year period, an average of 45 per year. Of these, 39% dug themselves out, 34% were extricated by survivors on the scene, and only 27% were recovered by organized rescue actions. The central fact is that people die very quickly when buried under snow (Figure 5). The successful rescue is the speedy one, and time lost means lives lost no matter how well organized or equipped the survivors or rescue parties are.

If someone is buried in an avalanche, prompt rescue operations are the only hope of getting the victim out alive. There are records of persons living several days while buried, but such instances are exceptional. Ordinarily the victim either is killed by mechanical injury, or dies within a short time from shock and suffocation. Some victims die within a few minutes from no obvious cause.

Two-thirds of avalanche fatalities are due to suffocation. Most of the remaining third are due to mechanical injuries, mainly to the head or neck.

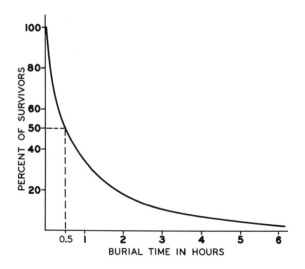

Fig. 5—Percent of survivors as a function of burial time for completely buried avalanche victims. After a paper by Knox Williams given at USFS Fifth National Avalanche School.

Earlier statistics suggested that about 50% of completely buried victims were still alive after the first hour. In recent years the rapidly expanding record of accidents exposes the mournful fact that the 50% survival time is actually closer to 30 minutes in North America, and about 45 minutes in Switzerland. In both areas, the chance of survival drops to less than 20% after 2 hours. Less than a third of completely buried victims are recovered alive.

Depth of burial is also critical. For burial depths of less than 1½ feet, the survival rate is around 45%. Only 1% survive burial at depths of more than 6 feet; at more than 9 feet there are no survivors.

Rescue operations which seek at least a 50-50 chance of success must therefore locate *and uncover* the victim within a half-hour. Once more the emphasis: *speed is crucial.*

But remember too, these figures are averages and exceptions can always occur. Special circumstances, like being trapped in an air pocket, can prolong a buried victim's life far beyond the averages, so rescue operations ought not to be abandoned until all reasonable hope of success is past.

Successful avalanche rescue operations depend on trained leadership, manpower, special equipment, and, above all, organization. Successful (and by definition, speedy) rescues can seldom be improvised on the spot. Proper equipment must be provided and organization established beforehand. Although volunteer manpower can often be recruited in an emergency, rescue teams must be led by persons who are trained in rescue techniques. Leaders must know how to sound an accident alarm, and where to locate volunteers and equipment. They must know the designated rally points where volunteers can be assembled and equipped. They should know details of the local terrain and the normal areas of avalanche hazard.

The rescue leader often is the most experienced person in an area. He does not necessarily lead by marching at the head of a rescue party, but by providing the organizational nucleus which holds a rescue operation together. He cannot function adequately without lines of communication—

telephones, radios, megaphones, runners. He appoints column leaders for rescue columns moving into the field, and ordinarily also designates one of the column leaders to be accident site commander. The latter directs the rescue measures at the accident site, unless for some reason the rescue leader decides to assume this function himself.

Modern avalanche rescue proceeds in three distinct stages.

Stage One — Location and Recovery of the Victim

Speed is the essential factor during this stage. Competent rescue personnel should reach the accident site with all possible haste. Subsequent organization of medical and logistic support is begun only after the first rescue parties have been dispatched.

1. On receipt of an accident alarm, the rescue leader calls for first-stage volunteers and appoints leaders for these groups. If the accident site is known accurately, the first groups leave immediately with all possible speed, equipped with probes, shovels, headlamps and, whenever possible, rescue transceivers for their own protection as well as victim search.

2. If witnesses remain at the accident site to guide the search groups, additional manpower is dispatched there as fast as it becomes available. If the person bringing word of the accident is the only witness, she should be returned to the site as fast as her physical condition permits in order to point out the victim's approach to the slide and the last-seen point.

3. At the avalanche the accident-site commander assumes charge of the search operations. He directs a search of the debris surface for clues and to mark key locations, such as the last-seen point. If the victim is known to be carrying a transceiver, the accident-site commander also directs an electronic search. He also initiates probing operations, when appropriate. The exact manner in which these will be done depends on the peculiarities of the avalanche, the number of buried victims, and the number of searchers at the site commander's disposal.

4. Once a quick visual check for clues has been completed, the rescue party begins coarse probing in the most likely locations. The coarse probe (Figure 6) moves rapidly. It is intended to locate the victim quickly at those depths of burial where he has the most chance of survival. If manpower permits, more than one coarse probe line may be in operation. These lines move fast enough to uncover clues to the debris surface as well as to probe for the buried victim.

5. Initial probing activities usually will concentrate on the most probable areas of burial, such as around trees, boulders, or other obstructions; where changes in slope occur, and at the tip and edges of the debris. If the last-seen point has been clearly marked, the search will further concentrate in the natural flow line downhill from this point.

6. The coarse probe does not guarantee locating the victim alive at a given spot, but statistical analysis shows that the increase of speed over the fine probe improves the victim's chance of survival. The fine probe virtually guarantees the victim will be found if he is not buried below the probe

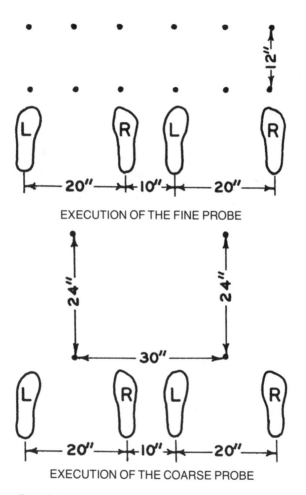

EXECUTION OF THE FINE PROBE

EXECUTION OF THE COARSE PROBE

Fig. 6—Fine and coarse probing techniques to search for a buried victim

depth, but there is a much greater chance that he will be found dead. Analysis further shows that the victim's chance of survival is also better if the coarse probe is repeated when it fails to find him on the first sweep. The statistical advantage of the coarse probe over the fine probe increases as the size of the search area goes up.

7. Because the fine probe is so much slower than the coarse one, it will normally be introduced only after the chances of live rescue have become small. Fine probing may take several hours to cover the likely burial spots in a large avalanche. It is usually intended to recover a body rather than to rescue a living victim.

8. With either type of probing, a separate shovel crew normally follows the probe line. If a strike is made, the probe pole is left in contact with the buried object, while the rest of the probe line moves on. The shovel crew then digs out the strike without interrupting the continued search, thus wasting no time if the strike does not turn out to be the victim.

9. Normal precautions during the rescue include posting an avalanche guard if danger from other slopes still exists, dispatching or radioing reports to the rescue leader on search progress and needs, and maintaining a close control over search parties to ensure that searchers do not fall exhausted, become lost, or wander into an avalanche danger zone. This last precaution is especially important at night.

10. The preceding steps assume the rescue team will travel on the ground to the accident scene. In many areas helicopters are available, which greatly improve the speed of rescue. They also improve safety by transporting the rescuers without exposing them to avalanche danger en

route, although care must be taken when approaching the accident site because it is possible for the downdraft from the helicopter rotor to start other avalanches in unstable snow. Trained rescue groups can benefit from practice with helicopter transport to ensure maximum safety and minimum lost time during an actual rescue. Helicopter evacuation of recovered victims is especially valuable because they can often be taken directly to a hospital. As demonstrated by current experience, the combination of radio communication, electronic rescue transceivers, and helicopters can lead to very rapid recovery of buried avalanche victims. In some cases, though, the record of live recovery has improved little owing to the time required to dig out deeply buried victims. The victim's best chances still lie with immediate recovery by the survivors on site as soon as the avalanche comes to rest.

Stage Two — First Aid and Transport of the Victim

1. As soon as the Stage One columns have been dispatched, the rescue leader organizes a first aid column, which should include a medical doctor whenever possible. This column carries first aid and resuscitation supplies, shelter, sources of heat, and facilities such as a toboggan to transport the victim. Allowing for extra time to open central caches, procure equipment, and collect personnel, the first aid column must also move with speed. Prompt, effective first aid is almost as essential to the victim's survival as his disinterment from the snow.

2. Because suffocation is a major medical fac-

tor for avalanche victims, the provision of resuscitation equipment is necessary. Mouth-to-mouth resuscitation is the first step to revival and should be applied as soon as the victim's head and chest are uncovered. Be careful at this point; mechanical injury of the head and neck may be present and could be worsened by rough handling. Prolonged artificial respiration is exhausting to the operator, especially at high altitudes. Modern, hand-operated resuscitators provide more reliable and controlled ventilation of the victim's lungs with intubation, but do have limitations. At low temperatures common to avalanche rescues, icing may give trouble with the valves. Much more important, the resuscitator pumps cold external air into the lungs and causes further chilling of an often hypothermic victim. Equipment to deliver warmed, humidified air for field treatment of hypothermia is a very useful adjunct to avalanche rescues. Oxygen may also be supplied (the resuscitators usually have a fitting for this), but is not essential except at very high altitudes. Prompt and steady artificial respiration is the essential provision.

3. Current medical opinion in the U.S. and Europe recommends cardiopulmonary resuscitation (CPR) for avalanche victims who exhibit absence of both breath and pulse. In this situation, prompt, steady application of CPR without interruption is important. CPR should be done only by persons trained in the technique, and training in CPR should be undertaken by as many prospective members of a rescue party as possible.

4. All victims recovered from avalanches should be assumed to suffer from hypothermia and handled accordingly. Once a victim is recov-

ered with breathing and pulse restored, the danger is not over. Hypothermia poses a threat to life that persists after excavation from the snow. Body temperature may continue to fall during transport, possibly cooling the heart to a point where fatal fibrillation may occur, as cold blood from the extremities mixes with warmer blood in the body core. Allowing a victim to walk speeds this process and may result in his collapse. Beware of this "rescue death."

The heart of a cold victim is irritable and sensitive to jarring. Rough handling of a severely cold victim may cause the heart to stop or beat irregularly. Gentle treatment is essential. Clothes should be cut off rather than pulled or jerked. Make every effort to insulate the victim from the cold and to rewarm *gently*.

If breathing and pulse are lost during transport, continue resuscitation efforts until the victim has reached a hospital. Many victims who appear pulseless while cold have been successfully resuscitated once warm.

All winter travelers in the mountains should learn the hazards of hypothermia and the correct ways of dealing with them. Any serious avalanche rescue is likely to involve hypothermic persons, quite possibly among the rescuers as well as the victims!

5. Once the victim has been revived, or breathing restored, he must be watched carefully during transport for subsequent cessation of breathing or pulse. Resuscitation in this case must be initiated immediately. Mechanical injuries are handled according to standard first aid techniques. Transport follows normal procedure for winter

accident victims.

6. Provision of adequate first aid and resuscitation supplies in rescue caches builds the foundation for successful rescue work. The care and handling of the victim after recovery cannot be too strongly emphasized. The rescuer's job is only half done when the victim is found.

Stage Three — Logistic Support for Prolonged Rescues

1. In the event of a deeply buried victim, several victims, or a large avalanche, the search may become prolonged. Additional support for the rescue workers will be needed. Once he has dispatched the search and first aid columns, the rescue leader can turn his attention to organizing relief manpower, supplies of food and clothing, transport (e.g., helicopters or oversnow vehicles), better lighting for night work, and reliable communications with the accident site. Such work normally brings the rescue action under the cognizance of civil authorities.

2. Systematic fine probing is arduous work, especially in hard snow. It is also destructive to all but the stoutest probe rods. Provision of relief for the probing parties is necessary if the search becomes prolonged. Adequate supplies need to be delivered to the site. There normally is some leeway in organizing such support, but even so, the first relief groups should be arriving at the accident site within 2 or 3 hours after the first rescue columns.

3. If systematic fine probing fails to locate the victim, then trenching of the snow is usually necessary. This is a major shoveling operation,

which can go on for many hours, or even days. It obviously is aimed at recovering a body rather than effecting a live rescue. Trenches are dug parallel to the slope contours down to ground level or to undisturbed snow. The walls between the trenches are probed laterally. Normal trench spacing is 6 feet, but this can be increased to 10 if sectional probes are available. Digging can also begin at the tip of debris cones and proceed uphill. It is best to space the shovel crews along one trench, with frequent reliefs. In this way snow from one trench can be thrown into the one just completed.

Avalanche Rescue Caches

Careful advance planning and preparation are essential to orderly and effective rescue. Avalanche rescue caches equipped with necessary supplies should be placed at readily accessible points in areas of high avalanche hazard. All caches should contain as a minimum for each departing group of rescuers:

> Collapsible avalanche probes
> Avalanche cords
> Climbing skins
> Climbing rope
> Headlamps
> Portable two-way radio

The following specialized equipment is required during the main stages of rescue:

Stage I— Avalanche probes (thin-wall *steel* tubing is by far the best)
First aid kit
Resuscitator
Filament tape and nylon cord

Shovel pack containing
  D-handle aluminum shovels
  wands or flags
  ball of cord or heavy string
  flares
  area map and compass
Stage II— Resuscitator
  Oxygen
  First aid kit
  Physician's medical kit
  Sectional toboggans
  Winter sleeping bags
  First aid tent
  Portable stove
Stage III—Avalanche probes
  Portable stoves
  Flares
  Portable floodlights
  Blankets
  Food
  Sleeping bags
  Tent
  Extra clothing

These suggestions are the bare minimum. Additional equipment such as an electronic megaphone is also useful. Whenever feasible, rescue parties can gain added safety by carrying electronic rescue transceivers.

The following is minimum equipment that should be available at all times in a central location at ski and climbing areas in avalanche terrain:

12 probes (sectional preferred; otherwise, metal rods or tubes ½″ diameter, minimum 12′ long; thin-wall steel tubing is recommended)

12 snow shovels

12 electric headlamps; carton of spare batteries

100' climbing rope

First aid kit (standard ski patrolman's kit is satisfactory)

Toboggan with blankets (collapsible toboggan light enough to be backpacked is preferred)

The following additional equipment is recommended:

Emergency rations

Chemical hot pads for toboggan

Gasoline stoves

Camp cook kit

Mountain tent

Climbers

Gasoline lanterns

Portable two-way radio (USFS, Ski Patrol, etc.)

A Special Note on Shovels

For central avalanche caches, the best compromise between effective size and weight is the 12-inch aluminum grain scoop with D-handle. Several of these can be nested in a rucksack or on a pack frame for transport to the accident site. Prolonged digging in hard snow, however, is easier with a steel shovel. The flatter "coal and street cleaner's" model is effective but adds considerable weight. Larger shovels are more effective in soft, light snow, but take too large a bite for easily lifting and throwing in the dense snow characteristic of avalanche debris.

The recent rapid increase in ski touring and the

accompanying use of electronic rescue transceivers have called attention to the problems of shovels easily carried in a rucksack. The customary smaller models, which fold or break down for transport, are much better than hands or ski heels but still have serious limitations for rapid digging in a rescue. Of these, the plastic model sold by Snow Research Associates of Jackson, Wyoming has some edge in shoveling speed owing to its shape. More useful shovels are sometimes made by cutting off part of both blade and handle of an aluminum grain scoop and arranging a method of disconnecting blade from handle (e.g., Ramer 08-014) for transport.

Avalanche Accident and Rescue Report

The following report outline is designed to furnish legal and statistical information to civil authorities. It is not suitable for medical personnel reporting details of the victim's condition.

1. Date, time, and location of accident

2. Names of victims and other members of party, along with information about their mountain and avalanche experience

3. Summary of events leading to accident: departure point, route, and destination or objective

4. Eyewitness account of accident, if available; otherwise, observer's deductions based on tracks and any other evidence; important points: location of skier in relation to release point of slide; assessment of how slide was released

5. Summary of rescue operations (times and names are important):

Time of accident

Time accident reported and by whom

Time first party dispatched and name of leader. Number in party

Time of first party's arrival at accident site

Procedure at site

Time victim is found

Location of victim at time of discovery

Injuries sustained by victim

Cause of death, or other outcome

Time operation concluded

6. Weather and avalanche background: wind, temperature, and snow data; avalanche restrictions in force, if any; type of slide and extent

7. Terrain data, including maps and diagrams

8. Recommendations and conclusions

Send a copy of the report to

Westwide Avalanche Data Network
c/o Colorado Avalanche Information Center
10230 Smith Road
Denver, Colorado 80239

TECHNICAL AIDS TO LOCATING A VICTIM

Several methods have been used to locate buried avalanche victims, and many more have been proposed. All fall into two basic categories: those that require the victim to carry some kind of active or passive signaling device and those that do not. Following is a summary of the various possible search methods:

I. Victim carries no signaling device
    A. sense mechanical permeability (probe)
    B. chemical emissions or scent (dog)
    C. detection equipment to sense

1. heat emission
2. sound emission or reflection
3. radar reflection
4. dielectric effects
5. light reflection (laser)
6. gravitational effects

II. Victim carries a signaling device
   A. passive device
      1. radar reflector
      2. radar transponder
      3. metal object
      4. permanent magnet
   B. active device
      1. radioactive source
      2. chemical source
      3. electromagnetic transmitter
      4. mechanical signal (avalanche cord)

Several of these methods, such as heat emission, gravitational effects, or light reflection, are more or less theoretical. For these, there are too many practical problems with the physical properties of snow, very marginal detectability, and requirements for complex equipment. Radioactive detection works nicely, but only with sources strong enough to be very dangerous to the bearer (and anyone else around). Portable search radars have been built which detect reflections from a buried body, but they are difficult to use because they also detect many spurious reflections. If the victim carries a radar transponder (frequency-doubling diode), search radars are much more effective. A radar system based on transponders has recently been introduced in Sweden, Italy, and Yugoslavia. A strong permanent magnet can readily be detected by a portable magnetometer, but the method has not gained wide favor owing to the high cost of this instrument and its limited search range.

No doubt new methods will be developed in the future. Recent reports from Europe, for instance, mention experiments with a chemical detection system called "Lawino," which could serve as an electronic dog. The need for speed, however, presents a basic, practical limitation for any complex device that must be transported from a central rescue station to an accident site. Any such device, no matter how effective, is more valuable in saving a rescue team's time in locating a body than it is in saving a life.

The time-honored methods of mechanical detection—the probe and avalanche cord—remain useful because of their simplicity. The avalanche dog is a superb search "device," but requires a complex organization for training, maintenance, and delivery to be effective. Electronic rescue transceivers have dominated search technology in the last decade for practical and technical reasons, but above all because they enable an *immediate search by survivors for a buried victim.* These four methods are discussed at more length below.

Avalanche Dogs

A well-trained avalanche dog, usually a German shepherd, is often a very effective means of locating a buried victim in many cases and is the only fast method for a victim who carries no signaling device. In Switzerland, over 27% of live victims in recent years have been located by dogs, more than by any other single method. But an extensive network of trained dogs, coupled with efficient transportation, is necessary for such success. In North America, the record of dog rescues is limited. Many past efforts here to train good avalanche dogs have failed because of the extended time and systematic effort required. More recently, a nucleus of good avalanche dogs has been developed largely through the efforts of search and rescue dog associations. Nevertheless, the big North American problem with avalanche search dogs remains one of transporting them to often remote accident sites in time to effect live rescues. On this continent, most successful dog searches to date have recovered dead bodies.

Even untrained dogs sometimes will instinctively seek out buried victims, especially if the victim is the dog's master. Rescue groups are well advised whenever possible to take along any robust, winter-conditioned dog.

Avalanche survivors can contribute to rescue success by keeping a search dog's capacities and limitations in mind. A trained dog can do a coarse search at the rate of about 4 to 5 acres per hour. It will locate most live victims regardless of burial depth or snow conditions. It will locate dead victims in porous snow up to 6 feet deep and in compact snow up to 3 feet deep. A dog may have trouble immediately after an avalanche comes to rest because the victim's scent takes a few minutes to diffuse through the snow to the surface. Normal foot traffic by searchers on the avalanche debris does no harm, though it is helpful to clear the search area a few minutes before the dog arrives. Other odor sources in the snow, such as buried animals or household debris, may distract the dog. (Do not urinate on the avalanche!)

Consult local ski areas or rescue-dog associations for current information on available trained dogs. The location and telephone contacts for local avalanche dog handlers can be prominently posted in avalanche caches to help speed rescue.

The Avalanche Cord

Following an avalanche cord is one technical means of locating an avalanche victim. The cord is commonly light in weight, made of red or orange nylon, and about 50 feet long. The traveler in avalanche terrain attaches one end around his waist and lets the full length of the cord trail behind him. The theory is that at least some part of the cord will float to the surface of the avalanche as it comes to rest and thereby provide a visible sign of the buried victim's location. Some commercial cords have small metal arrows attached every 3 feet or so to indicate which end of the cord to seek.

Avalanche cords do work, but they are not infallible, as some recent tests using dummies in real avalanches have proven. The cords have the advantages of simplicity, low cost, and reliability. Their disadvantages are inconvenience in use and a tendency to get tangled up with other party members, other avalanche cords, or trees and bushes. The latter problem is severe for a fast-moving skier below timberline, where much skiing is done in the interior ranges of North America. Part of the tangling problem can be minimized if the cord is carried rolled up like a ball of yarn and deployed when approaching avalanche terrain. This is done by tossing the ball to unroll it after the free end is attached to the bearer. In recent years the avalanche cord has been widely supplanted by electronic rescue transceivers, but it remains a useful adjunct to safe winter travel.

Avalanche Probes

The time-honored technical method for locating avalanche victims is the probe, a long, slender rod which enables a searcher to kinesthetically feel differences in resistance ("mechanical permeability") between snow and buried victim. (For information on executing search procedures with probes, see "Organized Rescue Actions" earlier in this chapter.)

Collapsible probes are a valuable adjunct for any backcountry winter traveler. They break down into sections and are assembled by a variety of means. Good aluminum alloy tube sections joined by a well-designed screw connector are widely used and convenient to carry. Several manufacturers provide useful models. They are good for work in soft snow but tend to be damaged by prolonged use in hard snow. Avoid any sectional probe, whatever the material, that is flexible enough to droop very far under its own weight; these are too readily deflected by snow lumps. A sturdy probe, the Lindemann model, consists of steel tube sections strung on a steel cable with a tensioning device at one end. These probes are quick to assemble and reliable but substantially heavier than other types of sectional probes.

Full-length probes, usually 8 to 12 feet long, are the standard equipment of rescue caches. They are usually brought into play when prolonged searches must be made, often in dense, hard avalanche debris. They must be stiff and strong, but not so large in diameter that pushing them into hard snow exhausts the rescuers. *Avoid aluminum probes* for this purpose. Repeated experience has shown that they will not stand up to prolonged work in hard snow. Especially avoid aluminum electrical conduit. Any serious probing in the debris of a real avalanche will quickly turn conduit into a pile of pretzels. The best probes are steel, preferably tempered thin-wall steel tubing ⅜-½ inch in outside diameter.

Probes can be hazardous to the buried victim. In soft snow the resistance of a human body can be readily felt by the prober. In very hard snow the "difference in mechanical permeability" of a body and the surrounding snow is slight. Cases exist where probing failed to find a victim who later was recovered by trenching and found perforated. Chances of serious injury to the victim can be reduced (not eliminated) by providing blunt tips on the probes.

Electronic Rescue Transceivers

The biggest innovation in avalanche rescue in recent years has been the introduction of electronic rescue transceivers. These devices carried by persons exposed to avalanche danger transmit an electromagnetic signal which can be picked up by another transceiver switched to the receive mode. The transmitting unit is located by tracking increases in the received signal strength. These devices afford a fast, effective means of locating someone buried in avalanche debris. Today they are universally used by snow safety professionals and are also becoming widely used by backcountry skiers.

The original transceiver was developed in the United States under the name of "Skadi." The Austrian "Pieps" soon followed, then later came the American "Echo." These three types are compatible, that is, one can be used to locate either of the other two. Parallel to this development the Swiss introduced the "Autophon," which works on a different frequency, followed later by the German "Redar" and others. The "Autophon" and "Redar" are compatible with each other, but *not* with the Skadi, Pieps, or Echo. This has led to some disastrous problems during avalanche rescues when two incompatible transceiver types were in use. The latest response to this compatibility problem has been a new generation of transceivers ("Ortovox," "Redar II," and "Pieps III") which simultaneously transmit (or receive) on *both* frequencies. A brief detour through this technical question is instructive.

The Skadi, Pieps, and Echo all operate at 2,275 Hz as audio-frequency induction transmitters. Their advantages are stability, freedom from interference or effects of intervening obstacles, and increased sensitivity of signal strength to changes in distance. The main disadvantage is limited range with the size of antenna (ferrite stick) that can be fitted in a small package. The Autophon and its successors operate at 457 kHz, a radio frequency. Their advantages are greater range with less power consumption, but interference is a bigger problem and stability is obtained only through greater manufacturing cost. The Skadi has an effective range of about 100 feet; the Autophon, about 200 feet.

New types of transceivers continue to appear,

working on one, the other, or both of these frequencies. Additional search systems have also been proposed using variations of radio transmission and direction finding. The new user of rescue transceivers should be careful to get a unit compatible with those carried by expected search units and should choose a model whose reliability has been proven by experience. The guidelines for transceiver use outlined below assume one of the 2,275 Hz units, which is the overwhelmingly dominant frequency used in the United States. Users traveling abroad need to be aware of the compatibility problem.

Rescue transceivers have already saved the lives of several avalanche victims, but they do not guarantee survival. The mountain traveler should have a clear understanding of what they can and cannot do. Rescue transceivers are a simple, effective, and reliable means of *locating another unit operating in the transmit mode.* They offer no guarantee that such a unit will be recovered attached to a live body. Accident records include several cases where the buried victim's position was determined within a few minutes by a rescue transceiver, but the dead body was only recovered after hours of shoveling. Some common-sense precautions when using rescue transceivers can greatly enhance safety in avalanche terrain:

1. Make sure the units have fresh batteries properly installed (Pieps, Echo) or an internal battery fully charged (Skadi). Use only alkaline batteries, which work much better than the regular kind at low temperatures.

2. Set the unit to "transmit" and turn it on. When a party sets out, check each unit by listening to it

with another unit set to "receive." This check at the start of each tour is important!

3. Carry the transmitting unit inside a shirt, suspended around the neck or otherwise securely attached. A high-speed avalanche can remove a surprising amount of clothing; be sure the transceiver is not apt to go with it. A unit carried in the rucksack is useless, for the rucksack is one of the first things you want to get rid of when caught in an avalanche.

4. Each person carrying a transceiver should also *carry an avalanche probe.* A survivor can switch his unit to "receive" and locate a buried victim's position within about 3-6 feet. The system will not tell how deep burial is or give the exact place to start digging. Once electronic location of the victim is accomplished, probe for the precise location and then dig down along the implanted probe.

5. Each person carrying a transceiver should also *carry an adequate shovel.* The importance of this rule cannot be overemphasized. You may locate a buried avalanche victim with great dispatch, but this affords little comfort if you have only your hands or the heel of a ski to dig with. The small portable shovels commonly used for winter mountaineering and ski touring are better than bare hands, but they are inadequate for really serious, fast digging when someone's life is at stake. (See the discussion of shovels following "Avalanche Rescue Caches.")

Practice the search procedure regularly. Don't wait until one of your party is buried to figure out how the rescue transceivers work. Follow the printed search technique furnished by the manufacturers of these units. Although these techniques differ in minor details, they all employ a systematic search pattern which closes in on the buried transmission with minimum lost motions. Do not run around at random on the avalanche debris; this can waste valuable time. Here is the basic procedure. (See Figure 7):

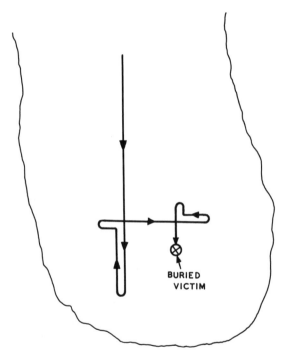

Fig. 7—A typical electronic transceiver search pattern to locate a buried victim

1. First, make a fast visual search of the debris field to see if there are any direct signs of the victim, such as a hand or foot protruding from the snow. Even an electronic search wastes valuable time if the victim can be located directly.

2. Switch *all* transceivers to the receive mode, extract earphones, and spread the survivors out into a search sweep of parallel lines about 100 feet apart. The fastest search occurs if terrain and party disposition after the accident permit a downhill search parallel to the fall line. If the victim's last-seen point is known, one of the search lines should follow the fall line down from this point. A single survivor should start the search along this line.

3. Once the buried transmitter signal is detected, continue along the search line until the point of maximum signal is reached. It usually will be necessary to go past this maximum point until the signal falls off, then return to it by retracing steps along the search line.

4. Determine by excursions in both directions at right angles to the initial search line which way the signal strength continues to increase, and move along a straight line in that direction until a signal maximum is again located.

5. Repeat the procedures again, moving at right angles to the second search line. This will usually bring the search very close to the victim. Scan the snow surface in this vicinity with the transceiver to locate the maximum signal, then use an avalanche probe to pinpoint the victim's location.

6. With Pieps or Skadi systems, as signal strengths increase during the search, keep turning

down the receiver volume control to keep the sound in the earphone to a low level (Echo does not provide volume control). This gives best aural sensitivity to changes in signal. The signal strength also depends in part on the orientation of the receiver antenna coil with respect to that of the transmitter. Once the search closes in on the transmitter location, experiment with receiver orientation to get the strongest signal, then maintain that orientation to finish the search.

7. If more than one victim is buried, searchers may hear two or more competing signals in their earphones. Try to concentrate on one signal at a time, locate it, and then work toward the next one. If the victims are buried far apart, different searchers may pick up the signals at different strengths and the problem will be quickly resolved. If the victims are buried close together, sorting the signals may require a slower scan of the snow surface to pinpoint individual locations. Backup work with avalanche probes may be necessary for closely adjacent victims.

CHAPTER FOUR
CASE HISTORIES

Reading about the mistakes of others is an effective way to learn how to avoid similar errors. That is why the previous edition of this handbook concluded with several case histories of avalanche accidents and rescue efforts. They have been removed from this edition because a much larger collection is now available elsewhere. In 1967, the U.S. Forest Service published *The Snowy Torrents,* edited by Dale Gallagher, a collection of accident case histories from the United States for the period 1910 to 1966. In 1975 a second volume of *Snowy Torrents,* edited by Knox Williams and covering the period 1967 to 1971, was published. A third volume, by Knox Williams and Betsy Armstrong, covering accidents from 1972 to 1979 appeared in 1984. The reader is strongly urged to consult these publications, study the case histories in detail, and take heed of the many ways in which the mountain traveler can fall victim to sliding snow.

The case histories that follow are of a different kind: they show how experienced people go about evaluating avalanche hazards, and they deal with a wide variety of snow conditions and hazard situations, all of the sort likely to be encountered by winter travelers in the backcountry.

Spring Ski Tour to Paradise Valley, Mount Rainier, April 1976

A ski touring trip was made to Paradise Valley after two days of clear weather had followed a spring snowstorm with substantial amounts of new snow at higher elevations on Mount Rainier. Circumstances were ideal for wet snow avalanches, with strong radiation on south exposures following new snow deposition. By the time Paradise was reached, it was obvious that little or no avalanching would occur that day:

1. Freezing level in the atmosphere was reported around 5900 ft, but little melt could be seen above 4900 ft. At the altitude of Paradise, about 5600 ft, there was limited snow melt even on slopes facing directly south.

2. The only observed avalanching on the second clear day after a spring snowfall was some wet snow activity on steep, forested slopes below 3900 ft. There was no activity at all on south exposures above 4900 ft, which was unusual for the season and snow conditions.

3. Glacier-fed Tahoma and Kautz Creeks were running clear, indicating that no prolonged melt had been taking place at higher altitudes.

4. New snow persisted on rocks at higher elevations on Mount Rainier in spite of the previous sunny days, again suggesting little or no melt.

5. The snow was very bright in the sunlight, indicating a high reflectivity characteristic of a snow surface with little or no liquid water present.

During the course of the ski tour to an altitude of about 8200 ft, further observations confirmed the original impression:

6. Surface snow was cold and underlying

layers poorly consolidated on shaded and north slopes.

7. By noon, many slopes showed the mirror-like gleam of firnspiegel, a very thin ice layer produced by a freezing snow surface during sunshine.

8. Local, patchy firnspiegel occurred everywhere underfoot above 5600 ft.

9. There was poor spring skiing (the original purpose of the tour as conceived in Seattle) with no corn snow development at all, even on the second day of hot spring sun.

Diverse observations over several hours had combined to form a picture of cool, dry air, which promoted snow surface evaporation and radiation cooling. This kept the snow surface mostly below freezing in spite of intense spring sunlight on south exposures. The dominant factor preventing normal wet snow spring avalanches was low atmospheric humidity at these altitudes. This could not easily be measured directly (the nearest Weather Service radiosonde station is at Quillayute, 150 miles to the northwest), but it could be clearly inferred from several lines of evidence about snow behavior.

Training Course in the Cariboo Mountains of B.C., January 1976

A training course in avalanche safety was planned for helicopter ski guides. In preparation for this course, a prior evaluation of avalanche conditions in the Cariboos was made, then refined after field observations on subsequent days. The preparation began a month in advance by studying weather reports for the Cariboo area.

1. Before the instructor left Seattle, recent

storm track data affecting the Cariboo area were reviewed. Storms were identified as light and few, indicating a thin snow cover with general TG metamorphism to be expected.

2. Valley snow depths observed during the train ride to Valemount varied from 18 inches at Blue River to 6 inches or less at Valemount. Clear effects were seen of rain on snow followed by 2 to 4 inches of new snow, plus general evidence of recent thaw followed by refreezing.

3. During the evening in Valemount, conversations with guides and a helicopter pilot pieced together the picture of a thin snow cover with the last significant snowfall having occurred over a week previously. A subsequent warm period with melt was followed by cold, windy weather. Recent natural avalanches had fallen, mostly from drift areas on high, lee slopes. Current conditions offered good powder skiing mixed with surface crusts and 2-3 inches of surface hoar on some slopes.

Already a picture of snow and avalanche conditions had emerged without the forecaster ever having set foot on the Cariboo slopes. An estimate of stability was then prepared on evidence to that point:

First Estimate: A shallow, erratically unstable snow cover with mixed layering, moderate to advanced TG snow, thaw crust up to 6900 ft, and a tricky and uneven hazard from lee-slope drifts above timberline. Extensive hazard could be expected from loading by any appreciable amounts of new snow.

On the next day, avalanche release zones were visited by helicopter, and test pits were dug to collect information about snow cover structure.

4. Snow depths averaged 30-36 inches with a weak structure involving much TG snow plus depth hoar in some places. In areas of deeper drifts, up to 80 inches thick, the snow cover was stronger, but with some TG snow at the bottom.

5. Skiing and some shallow, hasty pits confirmed these findings. The snow cover was shallow except in drift areas and generally showed advanced TG development.

At the end of this day of field investigation, a second stability estimate was made, based on direct observation of snow cover structure.

Second Estimate: Little change from first estimate. Snow marginally stable and likely to react to any kind of loading. Some present danger on slopes steeper than 40°, especially in drift areas.

The stability evaluation continued for a second day with a wide-ranging reconnaissance by skiing on slopes of varied altitudes and aspects. Test skiing on small, safe slopes was an important part of this evaluation.

6. Snow cover depth was broadly 25-30 inches, with depth hoar consistently appearing at the bottom.

7. A shallow layer of new snow on top of an old slab avalanche bed surface, the ground, had already converted entirely to very unstable depth hoar.

8. Surface hoar existed on some northeast slopes up to 1½-2 inches thick with a thin layer of new snow on top. This would become dangerously unstable with subsequent loading.

9. Numerous very shallow soft slab avalanches had appeared since the previous day among steep

rocks and gullies at higher elevations. These had likely been generated by continuing TG metamorphism in the recent new snow and were warnings of a developing weak snow surface which would poorly support the next snowfall.

The training group had been skiing very cautiously under these conditions and a consensus had developed among several experienced hands that snow conditions were tricky and could be locally dangerous. At the end of the second day in the field, a final stability evaluation was made.

Final Estimate: Essentially the same as the previous day's estimate. Even a moderate snowfall would create very unstable snow conditions awaiting the triggering action of a skier. A heavy snowfall would actually be safer, once the expected avalanche cycle was over, for it would clean out most steep slopes through natural avalanche releases.

In this case history, the estimate of avalanche danger progressed logically, starting with a broad judgment based on meteorological conditions and proceeding through an examination of snow structure to ski tests of the snow cover's actual mechanical stability. Each successive step added increasingly specific knowledge about snow stability, raising confidence in the accuracy of the original judgment.

Avalanches in Banff National Park, March 1977

In this example, forecasters were able to predict a very dangerous condition following a seemingly harmless snowstorm because they had paid close attention to the evolution of snow cover structure throughout the winter of 1976-1977, one of unusually light snowfalls in the Canadian Rockies.

1. December brought very light snowfalls, yielding a very shallow snow cover with extensive TG metamorphism.

2. The same conditions persisted into January. Depth hoar formation was extensive. Widespread avalanching following any heavy snowfall was already being predicted.

3. The same weather pattern continued into February. Toward the middle of the month an episode of surface hoar formation was widely observed in the Canadian Rockies. This layer of highly unstable crystals was subsequently buried by light snowfalls.

4. The light winter continued on into March, with some improvements in snow quantities. Skiers were frequently involved in avalanche accidents, with 13 separate incidents having occurred around the Sunshine ski area by late March. New avalanches were forming with snowfalls of as little as 1 to 2 inches.

5. There were 7 avalanche fatalities after mid-March in the Canadian Rockies and adjacent ranges. The February surface hoar layer appeared to have been the major cause of these accidents.

6. A storm arrived in the Banff-Sunshine area early on March 26. By the morning of the 27th, 10 inches of snow had fallen, and the wind was averaging 10 mph. The Banff Warden staff issued a public warning of extreme avalanche hazard, labeling some slopes as "suicidal."

7. The storm continued until evening of the 27th. A major avalanche cycle developed during the afternoon, with many large, natural releases

between 2:00 and 3:00 p.m. Many skiers in the Banff-Sunshine area failed to heed the warnings. Nine persons were caught in avalanches, 4 were injured, and 1 died.

By usual mountain weather standards, this late-March storm was almost trivial, with 13 inches total snowfall spread out over a 40-hour period. Many such storms occur in most areas each year without causing such extensive avalanching, but in this case an extremely unstable structure in the shallow snow cover was ready to react to even this modest loading. By following the winter-long evolution of the snow cover and noting the accumulating evidence from earlier avalanches, forecasters were able to anticipate very accurately what was going to happen. This was a situation where, clearly, "the forecast began with the first snowfall of winter."

Six Events in the Cascade Mountains

The following is a compilation of snow conditions which led up to six avalanche accidents or events at different times. In this instance the source is not an experienced avalanche hand but the Seattle newspapers, which often report avalanche accidents on the front page and with prominent headlines. An instructive common theme runs through these stories, connected by the incidental mention of snow and weather.

1. "...more than a foot of new, wet snow fell yesterday. The National Weather Service had a travelers' warning out with extreme avalanche danger in the Cascades. They forecast heavy snow through today..."

2. "Numerous slides were reported in the park

as warm, rainy weather hit the area yesterday....
gale winds, rain, sleet and snow raked the mountain yesterday..."

3. "Eleven inches of snow fell at the pass overnight....The Forest Service warned that an extreme avalanche hazard existed in the mountains. ...The slides were caused by a sudden warming that raised the freezing level to about 4500 ft."

4. "'Avalanche warnings were ignored,' he said. 'We just didn't check the conditions'...conditions that turned worse from morning rain and midday sun on the wet, heavy snow."

5. "The Forest Service had posted a high avalanche hazard for the Cascade Mountains over the weekend because of heavy snowfall. Eighteen inches of new snow fell in the 3 days before the avalanche."

6. (Report of an August mountaineering accident.) "'There was a high-pressure ridge growing and a declining chance of rain. We decided it looked feasible,' (survivor)....'But we've had 18 inches of fresh snow in the area in the past week, and there was a sheet avalanche up there that just gave way,' (investigator)."

Many avalanches in the Cascades are precipitated by obvious meteorological causes, most prominently a heavy fall of new snow or a sudden rain or thaw. A combination of new snow followed immediately by thaw or rain is even more effective. Weather forecasts and warning bulletins usually give from 12 to 36 hours notice of such events. By following weather evolution a day or two prior to a trip, or at least checking on hazard warnings the day of departure, winter recreationists can be apprised of dangerous conditions. If there is an avalanche information service in the area, it should be consulted. Close attention in the field can also help one recognize the rapid onset of danger. A drastic increase in snowfall, a sudden temperature rise, or rain starting to fall on cold snow can very quickly alter snow stability for the worse.

A Week of Ski Touring on the Ruth Glacier (Mount McKinley), April 1983

The occasion was a planned week of ski touring among the peaks surrounding the Ruth Glacier. This is a remote area, where no weather or avalanche reports are available and only the most general weather patterns can be deduced. Close attention has to be paid to whatever field evidence of snow stability can be obtained as the trip evolves.

1. Winter had lingered late in the Alaska range, and the usual April periods of fair weather had not yet appeared. Recent new snow and cold conditions were to be expected.

2. On the ski plane flight from Talkeetna a careful observation of how the snow lay on the mountains showed no evidence of recent, major avalanches except for isolated glacier icefalls. Fresh sluffs and small avalanches were scattered on very steep slopes. The snow-covered glacier surfaces showed evidence of only light wind drifting, but there was substantial cornice formation on the ridges.

3. An initial snow structure check was made while setting up camp on the glacier. A quick pit about 5 feet deep showed cold, unconsolidated snow in the top layers with solid, well-bonded older snow at depth. A quick shovel test did not reveal

any seriously weak shear planes.

4. A short ski tour to adjacent slopes identified weak snow layers to a depth of 18 to 24 inches, with some light surface slabbing on windward slopes.

First Estimate: Plenty of unsettled, recent new snow, with likelihood of soft slab development higher on the ridges. Degree of instability still unknown. Be very cautious!

Intermittent snow fell over the next three days, at times accompanied by strong winds and near-blizzard conditions. One to two feet of new snow accumulated during this period. There was no safe, reliable place to find a test slope in these poor weather conditions. Snow stability was expected to get worse with the snowfalls and wind drifting, so great caution was required. Some actual avalanches needed to be observed to confirm this judgment.

5. A slope near camp avalanched, possibly triggered by a mild earthquake. The dust cloud and light wind blast reached the campsite.

6. Clearing weather revealed that several soft slab avalanches had run from the higher ridge crests. An actual fall was witnessed.

7. A climbing party arrived in the area after an attempt on a nearby peak. They reported that while high in a couloir they encountered difficult going in deep, soft snow over a wind crust. On their descent they narrowly escaped being caught when this entire couloir avalanched.

Final Estimate: A marginal avalanche situation had rapidly evolved to a dangerous one with additional snowfalls. The meteorological evidence had pointed to this and was confirmed by observed avalanche falls. This was no time to be playing around on the steep slopes and ridges. Ski touring would be confined to gentle glacier slopes.

In a situation like this the avalanche danger could not be assessed beforehand, but had to be judged by a continuous appraisal of current conditions as the trip progressed. It is essential to be alert to different lines of evidence and to be very cautious until clear information turns up on what the snow stability is really like.

SUMMARY

These case histories have a common theme: avalanche forecasting as an ongoing process. The time spans involved are diverse, ranging from hours through a few days to an entire winter. In each case, evidence about snow stability is collected early, then continually supplemented with evidence from many additional sources. Progressive estimates of avalanche danger are made, each revising and improving on the previous one. The meteorological evidence (Class III) is often the starting point, providing a general appraisal of snow conditions. As the process evolves, more and more Class II and Class I evidence is sought to support increasingly specific estimates of avalanche danger. Observations or reports of actual avalanche occurrences provide solid confirmation about decreasing snow stability. The final decisions are based on a chain of evidence that progressively clarifies the initial uncertainties.

There is no one formula that will identify avalanche danger, no magic box that will flash a warning light when the snow is unstable. Reaching a clear evaluation requires constant attention and analysis. The practitioners in these examples were all doing what had become a habit: *They were always thinking about snow conditions.* It's a habit worth adopting, for survival often depends on it.

A SHORT BIBLIOGRAPHY OF AVALANCHE LITERATURE

Avalanche Atlas, International Commission on Snow and Ice of the International Association of Hydrologic Sciences. UNESCO, Paris, 1981.

The Avalanche Hunters, by Montgomery M. Atwater, McCrae Smith Company, Philadelphia, 1968.

Avalanche Safety for Skiers and Climbers, by Tony Daffern, Rocky Mountain Books, Calgary, 1983.

Avalanches and Snow Safety, by Colin Fraser, Charles Scribner's Sons, New York, 1978.

"Avalanches," by Malcolm Mellor, *Cold Regions Science and Engineering,* Part III, Section A3. U.S. Army CRREL, Hanover, N.H., May 1968.

Dept. of Agriculture Handbook No. 489, *Avalanche Handbook,* Washington, D.C., 1976. (Available from Government Printing Office.)

Field Guide to Snow Crystals, by Edward R. LaChapelle, University of Washington Press, Seattle and London, 1969.

Modern Avalanche Rescue, Snow Safety Guide No. 1, U.S. Forest Service Alta Avalanche Study Center, Alta, Utah, April 1968.

Mountaineering — The Freedom of the Hills, Fourth Edition, edited by Ed Peters, The Mountaineers, Seattle, 1982.

Snow and Its Metamorphism. Snow, Ice & Permafrost Research Establishment Translation No. 14, U.S. Army Corps of Engineers. (A translation of a basic text in snow mechanics published in Switzerland in 1939. Not widely available but may be found in some libraries.)

Snow Sense — A Guide to Evaluating Avalanche Hazard, by Jill Fredston and Doug Fesler. Division of Parks and Outdoor Recreation, Alaska Department of Natural Resources, 1984.

Snow Structures and Ski Fields, by Gerald Seligman. (Scarce and hard to find, but beautifully illustrated and a basic text in the field. Photo-offset editions in limited quantities are sometimes available through the International Glaciological Society.)

The Snowy Torrents — Avalanche Accidents in the United States, 1910-1966, Dale Gallagher, Editor. U.S. Forest Service Alta Avalanche Study Center, Alta, Utah, 1967.

The Snowy Torrents — Avalanche Accidents in the United States, 1967-71, by Knox Williams. USDA Forest Service General Technical Report RM-8, 1975. Second edition published by Teton Bookshop Publishing Company, 1981.

The Snowy Torrents — Avalanche Accidents in the United States, 1972-79, by Knox Williams and Betsy Armstrong, Teton Bookshop Publishing Company, 1984.

(The first two volumes of this publication are presently reported out of print but may be obtained in libraries. The third volume may be ordered from the publisher at Box 1903, Jackson, Wyoming 83001.)

INDEX

Other books from The Mountaineers include:

MOUNTAINEERING: The Freedom of the Hills, 5th Edition, Don Graydon, editor. Most complete, up-to-date book in existence on the how-tos of roped climbing, wilderness mountaineering.

MEDICINE FOR MOUNTAINEERING, 4th Edition, James A. Wilkerson, M.D., editor. A handbook of medicine, compiled by physician-mountaineers, for remote-area situations where care for a victim of illness or accident must go well beyond first aid.

MOUNTAINEERING FIRST AID, 3rd Edition, Marty Lentz, Jan Carline, Steven Macdonald. Compact handbook for prevention and treatment for remote-area accidents, illnesses, where medical help will not be available.

CROSS-COUNTRY SKIING, 3rd Edition, Ned Gillette and John Dostal. Technique, equipment for skiing everything from track to backcountry. Many photos.

HYPOTHERMIA, FROSTBITE AND OTHER COLD INJURIES, James A. Wilkerson, Cameron C. Bangs, John S. Hayward. Experts describe symptoms, solutions, and prevention of hypothermia. Includes frostbite and immersion.

SNOWSHOEING, 3rd Edition, Gene Prater. How to select, use and care for snowshoes for all types of terrain and snow conditions, from flatland walking to mountain slopes.

Write for complete catalog of over 200 outdoor titles:

THE MOUNTAINEERS • Books
1011 S.W. Klickitat Way, Seattle WA 98134